HISTORY OF SPORTS

BOXING

Titles in the History of Sports series include:

- Baseball
- Basketball
- Car Racing
- Football
- Golf
- Hockey
- Soccer
- Tennis
- Track and Field
- Volleyball
- Wrestling

BOXING

BY JOHN F. GRABOWSKI

LUCENT
BOOKS

THOMSON
—★—
GALE

San Diego • Detroit • New York • San Francisco • Cleveland • New Haven, Conn. • Waterville, Maine • London • Munich

© 2004 by Lucent Books. Lucent Books is an imprint of The Gale Group, Inc.,
a division of Thomson Learning, Inc.

Lucent Books® and Thomson Learning™ are trademarks used herein under license.

For more information, contact
Lucent Books
27500 Drake Rd.
Farmington Hills, MI 48331-3535
Or you can visit our Internet site at http://www.gale.com

LIBRARY OF CONGRESS CATALOGING-IN-PUBLICATION DATA

Grabowski, John F.
    Boxing / by John F. Grabowski.
        p. cm. — (History of sports)
    Summary: Discusses the origins and evolution of the sport of boxing, as well as memo-
rable events and key personalities in the game's history.
      ISBN 1-59018-353-3 (hardback : alk. paper)
     1. Boxing—Juvenile literature. [1. Boxing.] I. Title. II. Series.
    GV1136.G73 2004
    796.83—dc22

                                         2003015980

Printed in the United States of America

Contents

FOREWORD

More than many areas of human endeavor, sports give us the opportunity to see the possibilities in our physical selves. As participants, we all too quickly find limits to how fast we can run, how high we can jump, how far and straight we can hit a golf ball. But as spectators we can surpass those limits as we view the accomplishments of others and see how fast, how smooth, and how strong a human being can be. We marvel at the gravity-defying leaps of a Michael Jordan as he strains towards a basketball hoop or at the dribbling of a Mia Hamm as she eludes defenders on the soccer field. We shake our heads in disbelief at the talents of a young Tiger Woods hitting an approach shot to the green or the speed of a Carl Lewis as he appears to glide around an Olympic track.

These are what the sports media call "the oohs and ahhs" of sports—the stuff of highlight reels and *Sports Illustrated* covers. But to understand a sport only in the context of its most artistic modern athletes is shortsighted, for it does little justice to the accomplishments of the athletes or to the sport itself. Far more wise is to view a sport as a continuum—a constantly moving, evolving process. On this continuum are not only the superstars of today, but the people who first played the sport, who thought about rules and strategies that would make it more challenging to play as well as a delight to watch.

Lucent Books' series, the History of Sports, provides such a continuum. Each book explores the development of a sport from its basic roots onward, and tries to answer questions that a reader might wonder about. Who were its first players, and what sorts of rules did the sport have then? What kinds of equipment were used in the beginning and what changes have taken place over the years?

Each title in the History of Sports also identifies key individuals in the sport's history—people whose leadership or skills have made a difference in the way the sport is played today. Included will be the easily recognized names, the Mia Hamms and the Sammy Sosas, the Wilt Chamberlains, and the Wilma Rudolphs. But there are also the names of past greats, people like baseball's King Kelly, soccer's Sir Stanley Matthews, and basketball's Hank Luisetti—who may be less familiar today, but were as synonymous with their sports at one time as the "oohs and ahhs" players of today.

Finally, the series looks at the aspects of a sport that are particularly important in its current point on the continuum. Baseball today is better understood knowing about salary caps and union negotiators. One cannot truly know modern soccer without knowing about the specter of fan violence at matches. And learning about the role of instant replay is critical to a thorough understanding of today's professional football games. In viewing a sport as a continuum, the strides that have been made along the way are that much more admirable. It is a richer view, and one that shows how yesterday's limits have been surpassed—and how the limits of today are the possibilities of athletes in the future.

The Sweet Science

Boxing is known as the sweet science, from A.J. Liebling's classic 1949 book on boxing by the same name. The phrase actually dates back much earlier, however. Liebling got it from Pierce Egan, who referred to the sport as "the sweet science of bruising"[1] in the 1812 edition of his collection of articles about boxing in eighteenth-century England called *Boxiana*. As writer Gregory Crosby points out, however, it "is rarely sweet and hardly a science, depending as it usually does more on the mastery of fear and withstanding of pain than on elaborate strategies of footwork and jabs."[2]

A Mysterious Fascination

Whatever the case, boxing still holds a fascination for a significant percentage of the sporting public. Perhaps that is because it epitomizes the American dream, the saga of a man trying to fight his way to a better life for himself and his family. When a fighter steps into the ring, he stands alone, nearly naked, risking life and limb in battle with another individual.

Boxers cannot count on their teammates to rally them to victory if their performance is below par. They do not have someone else to whom they can pass the ball or turn to when in trouble. They can only rely on their own perseverance, determination, and courage to help them overcome their opponent.

A Sport of Surprises with a Cast of Characters

Sportswriter Larry Merchant once called boxing the "theater of the unexpected."[3]

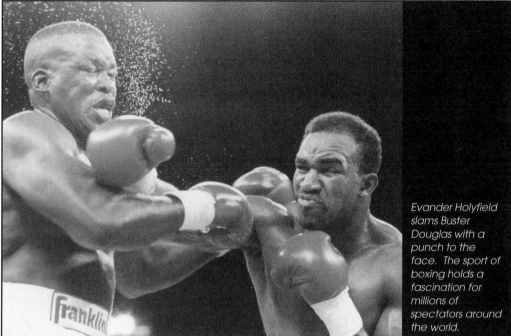

Evander Holyfield slams Buster Douglas with a punch to the face. The sport of boxing holds a fascination for millions of spectators around the world.

Although a bout consists of a limited number of rounds, a match can end at any time. All other sports must be played for a minimum number of innings, periods, sets, or holes. A fight, however, can end at any time, with an outcome that is totally unforeseen. One single punch—delivered to just the right spot at just the right moment with just the right amount of force— can help a fighter snatch victory from the jaws of defeat.

Boxing is also a sport of larger-than-life personalities. From John L. Sullivan to Stanley Ketchel to Muhammad Ali to Mike Tyson, the sport has had no shortage of controversial characters to capture the imagination—and interest—of fans

of all ages. Boxing extends across all national and political boundaries. With heavyweight title fights among the greatest of all sports spectacles, champions can become the most recognized athletes on the planet.

For these reasons, boxing will likely always hold a special fascination for fans everywhere. An athlete plays baseball or football or basketball or tennis or hockey or golf or any one of a dozen other sports. A person does not play boxing. The physicality gives it a special place in the world of sports. Boxing is about working hard to overcome and beat an opponent to the ground. To many people, it is viewed as a metaphor for life itself.

CHAPTER 1

Warriors All

Using the clenched fist as a means of protecting oneself is probably as old as mankind itself. When fighting eventually evolved into a sporting activity, bare knuckles remained the weapon of choice. Although early warriors sometimes used strips of leather to protect their hands, gloves did not come into vogue in boxing matches until mandated by the Queensberry Rules in 1867. The adoption of these rules removed much of the brutality from the sport and became the foundation for boxing as it is known today.

Ancient Warriors

Stone carvings indicate that boxing probably existed as early as 4000 B.C. in what is now Ethiopia. Egyptian hieroglyphics depict combat between soldiers whose arms and hands are braided in soft leather straps in a primitive precursor of the modern-day glove. The activity spread throughout the Mediterranean region, becoming popular among the early Greeks. A match between Epeus and Euryalus is described by Homer in the *Iliad:*

> Amid the circle now each champion stands,
> And poises high in air his iron hands,
> With clashing gauntlets now they fiercely close,
> Their crackling jaws re-echo to the blows,

And painful sweat from all their members flows.

At length Epeus dealt a weighty blow Full on the cheek of his unwary foe.

Beneath that ponderous arm's resistless sway.

Down dropped he, nerveless, and extended lay.

As a large fish, when winds and waters roar,

By some huge billow dash'd against the shore

Lies panting: not less batter'd with his wound

The bleeding hero pants upon the ground.[4]

The word *boxing* comes from the Greek *puxos*, meaning a box. It refers to the closed fist, which resembles a box in shape. *Puxos* was derived from *pugme*, a fist clenched for fighting. This becomes *pugilatus* in Latin, from which the English word *pugilism* has come to refer to the sport of boxing.

The pugilism found in Greece in 900 B.C. was different from the modern version of the sport. Two opponents sat facing

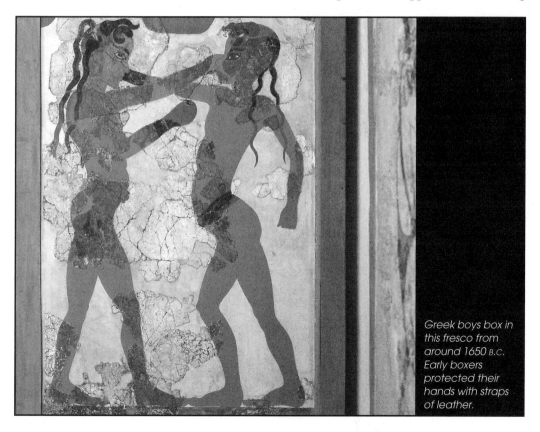

Greek boys box in this fresco from around 1650 B.C. Early boxers protected their hands with straps of leather.

each other on flat stones, their hands and forearms wrapped in soft leather thongs for protection. On signal, they began pummeling each other with blows until one was knocked unconscious or could not otherwise continue. Sometimes metal studs were embedded in the thongs, leading to even bloodier matches that often resulted in the death of one of the combatants.

Boxing made its debut in the ancient Olympics Games in 688 B.C. It was soon followed by the *pancratium*, a competition that combined boxing and wrestling. Combatants were allowed to do almost anything, short of biting and eye gouging, to defeat their opponent. Moves not allowed nowadays, such as kicking someone in the stomach, were perfectly legal.

Roman interest in the sport of boxing eventually led to its decline. The leather wrapping used by the Greeks was replaced by the cestus, which was made of harder leather and studded with pieces of metal or spikes. Too heavy to employ with a punching motion, the cestus was swung above the head and brought down with a hammering motion. The resulting carnage appealed to the bloodthirsty Romans, who flocked to see the death matches between slaves that were held for their entertainment. Common sense eventually prevailed, however, and the cestus was banned. With the threat of

death lessened, the sport declined in popularity. Boxing itself was finally outlawed in 30 B.C.

The Romans' most important contribution to boxing was the innovation of allowing the participants to maneuver within a fixed area, rather than having to remain relatively immobile. This area was the forerunner of the modern-day boxing ring.

THEAGENES OF THASOS

One of the most famous athletes of ancient Greece, Theagenes of Thasos, was a boxing champion in the seventy-fifth Olympiad (480 B.C.) and a *pankration* champion in the seventy-sixth Olympiad (476 B.C.). Such was his fame that, following his death, a large bronze statue was made in his honor. As the story goes, a longtime rival of Theagenes—who had never defeated him—used to come at night and beat the statue. One night it toppled over and killed him. Under Greek law all murders had to be punished, even if caused by an animal or inanimate object. The victim's sons prosecuted for murder, and the guilty statue was dropped into the ocean as retribution.

After a while famine and plague struck Thasos. When the people approached the oracle to find out what to do, the priestess told them to welcome back all exiles. Things reportedly did not return to normal until after Theagenes' statue was retrieved from its watery grave and repositioned in its original place.

The Cradle of Pugilism

Boxing as a sport disappeared over the ne__ __ousand year__. It made occasional a____ __ ___ __ _ recreation __n various ___ ___ ___ __ __urface as a ___ ___ _ century in England ____ __ __ __d to as the _ __Pugil___ __

___ ___ __ __ __ __ __ecame a pop-___ ____ ___ __ __fairs. Local ___ ___ ___ __ __ __age each other ___ ___ __ __lected from the ___ __ __ journalistic ref-___ __ __ __appeared in the ___ __ __January 1681:

___ ___ ___ tch of Boxing was performed __ __ __ His Grace the Duke of Albemarle, between the Duke's footman and a butcher. The latter won the prize, as he had done many times before, being accounted, though but a little man, the best at that exercise in England.[5]

Although boxing was illegal, the sport's popularity began to grow by leaps and bounds. By 1698 regularly scheduled matches were being held in the Royal Theatre in London.

A Code of Conduct

These seventeenth-century matches resembled modern-day wrestling as much as boxing. An opponent could be grabbed around the waist, lifted, and thrown to the ground or tossed over a shoulder in a move reminiscent of judo. Once his adversary was on the ground, the aggressor could then fall on him as heavily as possible. A round ended when a man was put down in such a manner. Following a thirty-second break, the fight continued. The match progressed until one man could not go on.

The action took place within a circle formed by a rope held by the spectators. The rope was eventually wound around a series of stakes inserted into the ground. Although there were no referees (the spectators made sure the rules were followed), a second outer ring was soon added to accommodate umpires, timekeepers, and whips, whose job it was to keep the crowd from becoming unruly.

The First Bare-Knuckle Champion

One of the strongmen who worked the village and town fairgrounds was James Figg (or Fig). Figg was born in Thame, Oxfordshire, in 1695. Six feet tall with a shaved head (so opponents could not grab him by the hair), he was an imposing figure. He became adept at all forms of man-to-man combat, including boxing and use of the backsword and quarterstaff. In 1719, at twenty-four years of age, Figg had defeated enough opponents to earn recognition as the first recorded champion of England.

That same year, Figg opened a fighting academy in London—Figg's Amphitheatre—where he taught "the noble science of defence."[6] The amphitheatre was one of several arenas in London where fights were staged. The ring in these arenas was an elevated square platform that was enclosed with wooden rails rather than rope. Such was the popularity of the sport that exhibitions attracted members of both the upper and working classes. After King George I attended one of the bouts, he sanctioned the construction of a "ring" in London's Hyde Park. With this royal sanction the sport began to gain some respectability.

The Father of Boxing

Figg won nearly three hundred matches in his career. He died at the age of thirty-nine in 1734 having retained his championship title for fifteen years. One of his students at his academy was Jack Broughton. Broughton eventually laid claim to the championship by defeating George Taylor, who had succeeded Figg. He was a more skillful fighter than Figg, relying on gambits such as blocking and counterpunching (immediately throwing a punch after blocking an opponent's attack) to overcome his opponents rather than brute strength.

In 1741 Broughton soundly defeated a Yorkshire coachman named George Stevenson. Stevenson was so badly battered that he died several days later. Upset by the tragedy, Broughton considered retiring. He decided against it and instead drew up a code of conduct for the sport in an effort to prevent further deaths. This code, published on August 16, 1743, came to be known as Broughton's Rules. It also helped earn Broughton the nickname "the Father of Boxing."

The First Written Rules

Broughton's Rules laid the groundwork for fair play in the sport of boxing. They were as follows:

1. That a square of a yard be chalked in the middle of the stage; and every fresh set-to after a fall, or being parted from the rails, each second is to bring his man to the side of the square, and place him opposite to the other, and till they are fairly set to at the lines, it shall not be lawful for one to strike the other.

2. That, in order to prevent any disputes, the time a man lies after a fall, if the second does not bring his man to the side of the square within the space of half a minute, he shall be deemed a beaten man.

3. That in every main battle, no person whatever shall be upon the stage except the principals and their seconds; the same rule to be observed in by-battles, except that in the latter, Mr. Broughton is allowed to be upon the stage to keep decorum, and

Roman Gladiatorial Combat

Roman gladiatorial contests evolved from the custom of sacrificing slaves at the funerals of notable figures. Eventually the slaves were given weapons and urged to defend themselves against their executioners. This soon was transformed into gladiatorial contests that were fought to the death. The matches became so popular that they were moved into large amphitheaters to accommodate the hordes who came to enjoy the "sport" of the event.

Roman gladiators became almost legendary for their bravery. In Joyce Carol Oates's book *On Boxing*, she mentions that according to Petronius, prior to battle Roman gladiators took the following oath: "We swear, after the dictation of Eumolpus, to suffer death by fire, bonds, stripes, and the sword; and whatever else Eumolpus may command, as true gladiators we bind ourselves body and mind to our master's service." Although most gladiators were slaves or condemned criminals, higher ranking freemen occasionally volunteered to compete. In even rarer instances, women took part.

A triumphant gladiator appeals to the crowd to decide whether his opponent should live or die.

to assist gentlemen in getting to their places, provided always he does not interfere in the battle; and whoever pretends to infringe these rules to be turned immediately out of the house. Everybody is to quit the stage as soon as the champions are stripped, before set-to.

4. That no champion be deemed beaten unless he fails coming up to the line in the limited time; or, that his own second declares him beaten. No second is to be allowed to ask his man's adversary any questions, or advise him to give out.

5. That in by-battles, the winning man to have two-thirds of the money given, which shall be publicly divided upon the stage notwithstanding any private agreements to the contrary.

6. That to prevent disputes in every main battle, the principals shall, on the coming on the stage, choose from among the gentlemen

Jack Broughton (left) trains with James Figg. Broughton created a code of conduct that laid the groundwork for fair play in boxing.

present, two umpires, who shall absolutely decide all disputes that may arise about the battle; and if the two umpires cannot agree, the said umpires to choose a third, who is to determine it.

7. That no person is to hit his adversary when he is down, to seize him by the hair, the breeches, or any part below the waist; a man on his knees to be reckoned down.[7]

Broughton's Rules were used throughout England, with only slight modifications, for nearly a century. They would be replaced by the London Prize Ring Rules in 1838.

Father of the English School of Boxing

Like many fighters of the day, Broughton had a patron, the duke of Cumberland. The duke brought him many members of the nobility who wished to learn how to fight. In order to protect them, Broughton invented "mufflers," or padded gloves, to prevent damage to his students' hands and to save them "the inconveniency of black eyes, broken jaws and bloody noses."[8] The mufflers were only used during sparring (practice or exhibition fighting); fights themselves were still bare-knuckle.

Broughton's boxing career came to an unceremonious end in 1750 following a match with a pugilist named Jack Slack. Broughton was the overwhelming favorite, and the duke of Cumberland wagered a good deal of money on him. A desperate punch to the forehead by Slack, however, caused Broughton's eyes to swell shut, temporarily blinding him. According to reports, the duke shouted at his fighter, "What are you about Broughton? You can't fight. You're beat." The courageous Broughton replied, "I can't see my man, Your Highness. I am blind, but not beat—only let me be placed before my antagonist and he shall not gain the day yet."[9] Despite Broughton's valiant efforts, however, Slack prevailed.

Broughton never fought again. He died at the age of eighty-five and was buried in Westminster Abbey in honor of his contributions to the sport. He is remembered today as "the Father of the English School of Boxing," and "the Father of the Science of the Art of Self-Defense."

Slack's reign as champion, in contrast, introduced an era of crookedness to the sport. With money being bet on the outcomes, gamblers occasionally fixed fights (offering fighters money to intentionally lose a match) to win their bets. The public lost interest and faith in boxing that was not restored until Tom Johnson (born Thomas Jackling) arrived on the scene in 1783. Johnson was a dignified, courageous champion who dominated the boxing world until 1791.

Scientific Boxing

Up to this point in time, there were no weight classes in boxing. The championship is often referred to as the heavyweight championship since the better fighters were usually the biggest and most powerful. Brute strength and endurance were the most desired qualities in a fighter of this era. All this changed when five-foot, seven-inch, 160-pound Daniel Mendoza came on the scene.

Mendoza was a Spanish English Jew from Aldgate, London. When he first took up boxing, he absorbed a great deal of punishment at the hands of a larger opponent. Determined not to suffer the same fate again, Mendoza devoted himself to what became known as the scientific style of boxing. He emphasized footwork, speed, and a left jab in his method, which depended more on guile and technique than on brute force. Mendoza reigned as champion from 1791 to 1795 and later became a respected boxing instructor, bringing his sport an unprecedented degree of respectability.

"Gentleman" John Jackson wrested the title from Mendoza in 1795 and continued the trend toward scientific boxing. When he retired, he opened a boxing academy in London. Among his many admirers was the famous poet Lord Byron, who referred to Jackson in a verse from his poem "Hints from Horace":

And men unpractised in exchanging knocks
Must go to Jackson ere they dare box.[10]

In an effort to bring some order to English prizefighting (fighting for money), Jackson established the Pugilistic Club, the first unofficial administrative body for English boxing, in 1814. The club, funded with money by its wealthy patrons, offered purses to boxers in an attempt to prevent them from taking bribes. It achieved limited success, however, before closing its doors a decade later.

Despite Jackson's attempt to legitimize the sport, prizefighting remained illegal, as it had been since 1750, and matches could not be advertised. Prize money could not be paid from the gate (the total admission receipts or attendance), since the number of spectators at a match could not be guaranteed. The money, therefore, had to be put up by the boxers themselves or by their backers. Since these backers were often members of the local aristocracy, there were few attempts made to prosecute the participants for participating in illegal prizefighting. (The participants were often "rewarded" by their backers, who made large sums of money betting on the fights.)

The London Prize Ring Rules

The next big move in an attempt to make the sport more honorable was triggered by an 1838 tragedy. That March, a fighter by the name of Bill Phelps died after

Daniel Mendoza (left) faces his opponent in a bare-knuckle match. Smaller than most boxers, Mendoza used footwork, speed, and guile to win fights.

being beaten in a fight with Owen Swift. In an attempt to prevent the recurrence of such a tragedy, Broughton's Rules were revised. The most important change required a fighter who was knocked down to return to the center of the ring unaided in order to resume the fight. This prevented seconds (a boxer's aides, who advise and care for him between rounds) from physically forcing a fighter to continue when he was in no shape to do so. The new regulations—which also prohibited kicking, gouging, butting, and intentionally falling to the ground in order to get a rest—became known as the London Prize Ring Rules. In the first championship fight held under the new rules, Deaf Burke lost his title to Bold Bendigo of Nottingham.

The First American Boxers

By this time, boxing had been introduced in the United States. It was first practiced illegally in the backrooms of taverns on the East Coast. The first two American boxers of note, Bill Richmond and Tom Molineaux, were slaves who earned their reputations in England. Known as "the Black Terror," Richmond was brought over by his master in 1777 when he was just fourteen years old. He had several noteworthy wins to his credit and eventually retired at the age of fifty-five.

Molineaux was given his freedom by his master and went to England in 1809. There he was trained by Richmond and became one of the country's top fighters. In 1810 he fought Tom Cribb for the championship, losing in thirty-nine rounds.

It was the first championship fight ever between black and white combatants. Pierce Egan—the first great sporting journalist—wrote of the bout:

> Molineaux proved himself as courageous a man as ever an adversary contended with . . . [Molineaux] astonished everyone, not only by his extraordinary power of hitting and his gigantic strength, but also by his acquaintance with the science, which was far greater than any had given him credit for.[11]

The rematch between the two men a year later—won by Cribb—is believed to have been the first sporting event to attract worldwide attention in the press.

EARLY BOXING NICKNAMES

Boxing fans have no trouble identifying modern-day fighters by their nicknames. Even the casual fan is familiar with Iron Mike (Mike Tyson), the Greatest (Muhammad Ali), Hands of Stone (Roberto Duran), the Brown Bomber (Joe Louis), and the Manassa Mauler (Jack Dempsey).

Only the hardened enthusiast, however, would be able to recognize names from the sport's early years. Some of these described a boxer's physical characteristics or temperament. Included in this category were the Deaf 'Un (James Burke), the Young Ruffian (Jack Fearby), and the Torkard Giant (Ben Caunt). Occupations or jobs accounted for "Nailer" Bill Stevens (blacksmith) and Jem "Black Diamond" Ward (who worked in a coal yard). Other nicknames were plays on a fighter's name (The Great Gun of Windsor for Tom Cannon and the Game Chicken for Henry—or Hen—Pearce).

Some nicknames, however, had a more unusual derivation. John Morrissey earned his reputation by fighting local toughs in the New York area. One such match against a scuffler named Tom McCann took place in an indoor pistol gallery under the St. Charles Hotel. At one point during the fight, Morrissey was pinned on his back over burning coals from an overturned stove. A

One of the legends of boxing, Jack Dempsey was nicknamed the Manassa Mauler.

cloud of steam and smoke—along with the smell of burning flesh—arose from Morrissey, but he refused to stop the fight. Somehow he managed to struggle to his feet and beat McCann. From that time on, he was known as Old Smoke.

Boxing in the United States

Boxing did not become popular in the United States until the early nineteenth century. The first real prizefight in the country in which the rules of boxing were observed is believed to have been a match between Jacob Hyer and Tom Beasley in New York City in 1816. America's first heavyweight champion was not declared until Hyer's son, Tom, defeated Yankee Sullivan in Rock Point, Maryland, thirty-three years later. News of Hyer's victory was wired to the New York newspapers, the first sports story sent over the wonderful new invention, the telegraph.

The sport continued to increase in popularity despite having received a setback in 1842 when a boxer named Tom McCoy died from injuries suffered in a 120-round bout with Chris Lilly. From that point on, prizefighting was strictly illegal in the United States. Matches were held nevertheless, as sympathetic politicians and officials declined to push for enforcement of the laws.

Boxing in America in the nineteenth century was dominated by fighters of Irish descent. Among the better-known boxers of the era were Yankee Sullivan (born John Ambrose), John Morrissey, and John C. Heenan. When Morrissey retired, Heenan became generally recognized as champion. A lack of worthy challengers for the crown in the United States led him to issue a challenge to English champion Tom Sayers for the "world title." The historic match—the first ever between champions of the two countries—was held on April 17, 1860, twenty-five miles outside of London, England. The hard-fought bout officially ended in a draw and championship belts were awarded to both participants.

Interest in boxing in England waned following the Sayers-Heenan match, in part because of the brutality of the fight. Politicians, police, and clergy alike became more determined to prevent matches from taking place than they had been in the past. It began to look as though prizefighting was doomed.

CHAPTER 2

The Queensberry Rules

Broughton's Rules had been in effect for almost a century before being supplanted by the London Prize Ring Rules in 1838. It was not until the Queensberry Rules were published in 1867, however, that boxing began to take on the form that is known today. The greater safety offered by the use of gloves and implementation of three-minute rounds was a significant step in transforming boxing from an illegal activity into a legitimate sport.

The Queensberry Rules

Following the Sayers-Heenan bout, it became obvious that changes had to be made for the sport to survive. Those changes came in the form of a new code set down by John Graham Chambers, a student at Cambridge University and a member of the London Amateur Athletic Club. Chambers wrote out twelve rules designed to eliminate most of the brutality from the sport. To publicize the rules, he sought out the patronage of John Sholto Douglas, the eighth marquis of Queensberry. Douglas agreed to sponsor the new regulations that came to bear his name.

The twelve Queensberry Rules—written in 1865 and published two years later—are essentially the rules of boxing in effect today:

1. To be a fair stand-up boxing match in a twenty-four foot ring, or as near that size as practicable.

2. No wrestling or hugging allowed.

3. The rounds to be of three minutes' duration, and one minute's time between rounds.

4. If either man fall through weakness or otherwise, he must get up unassisted, ten seconds to be allowed him to do so, the other man meanwhile to return to his corner and when the fallen man is on his legs the round is to be resumed, and continued till the three minutes have expired. If one man fails to come to the scratch in the ten seconds allowed, it shall be in the power of the referee to give his award in favour of the other man.

5. A man hanging on the ropes in a helpless state, with his toes off the ground, shall be considered down.

6. No seconds or any other person to be allowed in the ring during the rounds.

7. Should the contest be stopped by any unavoidable interference, the referee to name the time and place as soon as

John Sholto Douglas helped create the Queensberry Rules, a set of boxing rules still in effect today.

possible for finishing the contest; so that the match must be won and lost, unless the backers of both men agree to draw the stakes.

8. The gloves to be fair-sized boxing gloves of the best quality and new.

9. Should a glove burst, or come off, it must be replaced to the referee's satisfaction.

10. A man on one knee is considered down, and if struck is entitled to the stakes.

11. No shoes or boots with springs allowed.

12. The contest in all other respects to be governed by revised rules of the London Prize Ring.[12]

In addition to provisions for three-minute rounds, a ten-second count after a knockdown, and no wrestling, the most important change called for by the Queensberry Rules was the requirement that boxers wear gloves. Chambers intended his rules to be used in amateur bouts, such as those held at the London Amateur Athletic Club where he was a member.

The new rules were first used in an 1872 tournament where no prizes were awarded and no betting was allowed. Eventually they also were applied to pro-fessional matches. For a while, however, amateur bouts were held under the Queensberry Rules while prizefights continued on as bare-knuckle affairs.

The Boston Strong Boy

The Queensberry Rules became more respectable to bare-knuckle fans when the great English champion Jem Mace accepted them. With opposition to boxing having increased in England following the Sayers-Heenan fight, however, Mace and many of the other top fighters of the day went to the United States to continue their careers. Several men laid claim to the American title over the next few years. The championship became undisputed with Paddy Ryan's eighty-seven-round win over Joe Goss in 1880. Ryan lost the title in his very next fight when he was beaten by a powerful fighter by the name of John L. Sullivan from Roxbury, Massachusetts.

Known as the Boston Strong Boy, Sullivan became popular with the fans because of his powerful punching and his fun-loving, boisterous nature. He traveled around the country offering $100 to any man who could last four rounds with him. His popularity spread across the ocean to England, where he was greeted with enthusiasm when he fought several exhibitions there in 1887. After fighting a draw with English champion Charlie Mitchell in 1888 (the match was held in France since bare-knuckle fights were almost

MARATHON FIGHTS

Prior to the era of gloved fights and the Queensberry Rules, fights often lasted one hundred or more rounds. A fighter could extend the action by going down on one knee to earn a breather of thirty seconds before continuing.

After the Queensberry Rules, however, such marathon matches became rarer. The longest bout on record was the 110-round battle between Andy Bowen and Jack Burke on April 6–7, 1893, in New Orleans, Louisiana. The fight began at 9:15 P.M. on the sixth and did not end until 4:34 A.M. the next morning. The bout was called a draw after both fighters refused to come out for the next round, seven hours and nineteen minutes later. Three years earlier, Danny Needham and Patsy Kerrigan fought for six hours and thirty-nine minutes before their 100-round match was also called a draw.

The longest fight on record that went to a decision took place in Nameski, Illinois, on February 2, 1892. Harry Sharpe knocked out Frank Crosby in the seventy-seventh round of their meeting, putting an end to the festivities after five hours and six minutes.

impossible to stage in England), Sullivan returned to the United States.

The following year, Sullivan met Jake Kilrain, who had fought a draw with English champion Jem Smith. After beating Kilrain in a seventy-five-round match, Sullivan claimed the world title. The fight took its toll on Sullivan physically,

however, and he announced that he would no longer compete in any bare-knuckle bouts. In 1892 Sullivan put his title on the line against James J. Corbett. The match was the first bout for the heavyweight championship of the world under the Queensberry Rules. Not having fought in three years, Sullivan proved to be no match for Corbett. The challenger—a proponent of "scientific boxing"—eventually wore down the lumbering Sullivan, knocking him out in the twenty-first round to become the first Queensberry Rules champion.

The National Sporting Club

In England, meanwhile, boxing was beginning to take a step toward acceptability. Although the sport was still illegal, it had now gone indoors. Fights were held in public houses or sporting clubs under the Queensberry Rules.

One such venue was the exclusive Pelican Club, founded in 1887 by British aristocrats. Many consider the club to be the first semiofficial governing body of the boxing world. It soon closed down, however, and was replaced by the National Sporting Club (NSC), established in London in 1891.

Membership in the NSC included the aristocracy and many leaders of industry. As first president of the club, Hugh Cecil Lowtner (the fifth earl of Lonsdale) did his best to make the sport respectable.

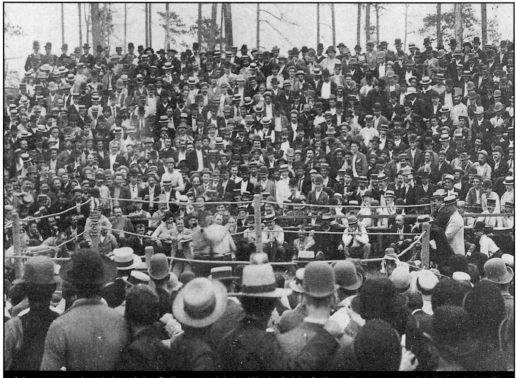

A large crowd watches John Sullivan and Jake Kilrain fight. Sullivan became world champion after defeating Kilrain in seventy-five rounds.

Matches came under strict control and were run with a high degree of decorum. More often than not, spectators wore evening dress. Silence was observed during the bout, with applause limited to the periods between rounds. In this way, those who bet on the match would have less influence on the referee, who officiated the match while sitting outside the ring wearing a top hat. Fighters were expected to adhere to co-owner John Fleming's belief that "Every boxer should try to overcome his adversary in a fair, manly and generous spirit, and bear in mind that there is more honour in losing like a gentleman than in winning like a blackguard."[13] The NSC quickly became a major force in English boxing, known throughout the world for promoting high-quality contests and for bringing a degree of legitimacy to the sport.

The Move Toward Respectability

Although boxing was still illegal in the United States, most bouts were tolerated, if not welcomed. New York finally became the first state to permit boxing with the passage of the Horton Law in 1896. The law was repealed four years later, however, after what was believed to be a fixed fight between James J. Corbett and Kid McCoy. It was replaced by the Lewis Law, which allowed fights between members of sanctioned boxing clubs.

The following year (1901), a bout between Jack Roberts and Billy Smith at the NSC in London led to a court decision that went in boxing's favor. Smith (his real name was Murray Livingstone) died as a result of injuries he suffered in the ring. Roberts and nine members of the NSC were charged with "feloniously killing and slaying"[14] Smith. Rather than putting the defendants in jail, the prosecution admitted that the reason for the suit was to put an end to boxing. Since the jury decided the death occurred in a properly regulated bout, however, it ruled it to be accidental and found the defendants not guilty. From that point on, the police concerned themselves with maintaining order at matches rather than worrying about their legality.

Weight Classes

The NSC emerged from the *Smith* case stronger than ever. It continued to work to help improve boxing's image and to regulate the sport. To this end, one of its most important moves was to establish standardized weight classes. Prior to this, there had been no clearly defined weight classes. Interest in boxing had centered around the heavyweights, but other matches paired off fighters of lesser weight. These categories became known as lightweights, middleweights, and, eventually, bantamweights, featherweights, welterweights, and flyweights. Among the best of these lighter fighters were middleweight Jack Dempsey (known as "the Nonpareil"), featherweight Albert Griffiths ("Young Griffo"), and bantamweight George Dixon ("Little Chocolate").

In 1909 the NSC announced the following limits for weight classes:

Flyweight	112 pounds
Bantamweight	118 pounds
Featherweight	126 pounds
Lightweight	135 pounds
Welterweight	147 pounds
Middleweight	160 pounds
Cruiserweight	175 pounds
Heavyweight	Over 175 pounds

The new classes quickly became accepted worldwide, except in the United States, where the 175-pound class was called light heavyweight. (The British switched to the American term in 1937.) To go along with the new classes, Lord Lonsdale—president of the NSC—donated ornate gold and enamel belts that were awarded to the champion of each division. In this way, the club was assured of having a monopoly on British championship matches.

The first Lonsdale Belt was won by lightweight Freddie Welsh in 1909. Other first winners included,

Flyweight: Sid Smith

Bantamweight: George Stanley

Featherweight: Jim Driscoll

Welterweight: Aschel Joseph

Middleweight: Tom Thomas

Cruiserweight: Dick Smith

Heavyweight: Billy Wells

The Color Line

By this time, boxing had begun to establish itself in many parts of the world. Interest in the sport had been fostered by its introduction into the 1904 Olympic Games in St. Louis, Missouri. In addition to being popular in England, Australia, and Canada, it was beginning to take hold in several other European countries. Most of the better boxers, however, came to America in their search for boxing fame and fortune.

Although the United States was the center of the boxing world, the sport largely ignored a significant segment of the population. Blacks were generally considered inferior to whites in every respect and whites generally refused to fight blacks. Since it was nearly impossible for the top black fighters to get matches against their white counterparts, they had to be satisfied with fighting each other time and again. One of the few ways they could make money was to take part in what were known as "battle royals." In these events, six or more fighters were put in a ring together. The last one standing was declared the winner.

One of the most successful of these black boxers was Jack Johnson. One of the top fighters of the era, Johnson did not get a title bout until 1908, when he fought champion Tommy Burns for the heavyweight crown in Sydney, Australia, at the age of thirty. Initially Burns avoided the match against Johnson. However, Australian boxing promoter Hugh D. McIntosh saw a great deal of money could be made from a matchup between a black and a white fighter. He offered Burns a great deal of money to fight, which Burns eventually accepted. Johnson went on to defeat Burns and, as the first recognized black champion, the flamboyant Johnson

THE GOLDEN GLOVES

The Golden Gloves was the brainchild of sports editor Arch Ward of the *Chicago Tribune*, the same man credited with the original concept for the major league baseball All-Star Game. Ward's idea was for a boxing tournament that would help the youth of the city and promote amateur boxing competition. The winner of each weight division received a small golden glove, giving the tournament its name.

The first competition, sponsored by the *Tribune*, was held in Chicago Stadium in 1923. Five years later, the *New York Daily News* began promoting a similar tourney on the East Coast. The winners of the two tournaments met in the Golden Gloves Tournament of Champions.

Originally intended for just local fighters, the two competitions began attracting youths from other towns. Eventually smaller tournaments were held in other cities, with the champions coming to Chicago and New York to compete in the super tournaments. The winners of these two meetings then vied for the national Golden Glove championships. Today the Tournament of Champions is held in a different city each year. Profits go toward advancing amateur boxing around the country.

The Golden Gloves plays a major role in the selection of boxers to represent the United States in the Olympics. Such stars as Joe Louis and Muhammad Ali launched their careers in the Golden Gloves.

Joe Louis (second from right) poses with the 1934 Golden Gloves champions. Many successful boxers launched their careers in the Golden Gloves.

quickly became one of the most hated men in segregated America. Former undefeated heavyweight champion James J. Jeffries was eventually persuaded to come out of retirement to face the despised Johnson.

In a match put together by famed promoter Tex Rickard, Johnson met Jeffries in Reno, Nevada, on July 4, 1910. The out-of-shape Jeffries was no match for the champion, and Johnson won by a knock-out in the fifteenth round. The black man's victory led to rioting in various parts of the country. Several people were killed, hundreds were injured, and thousands were arrested in the violence that erupted.

Johnson retained his title until losing a controversial bout to Jess Willard in 1915. It would be almost a quarter of a century until a black man was again allowed to fight for the heavyweight crown.

The No-Decision Era

Boxing's appeal during this period was hindered by the passage of the Frawley Law in 1911. The law limited bouts in New York State to ten rounds. In an attempt to stop fixed fights, it also forbade decisions, meaning that unless a match resulted in a knockout, it was officially recorded as a "no-decision." The reasoning behind this was that a fix was less likely if the only way to win was by knockout.

Under the Frawley Law, the referee could not name a winner of a fight. That did not, however, prevent newspapers from giving their opinion of the outcome (which came to be called a "newspaper decision"). By comparing different newspaper accounts, it was usually possible to determine who was the actual winner of a particular fight. When the Frawley Law was repealed in 1917 (probably due to unpopularity of the no-decisions), boxing again became illegal in the state.

The Walker Law

The next year, Englishman William A. Gavin arrived in New York and formed an organization based on England's National Sporting Club. Before he could begin operation, however, the sport had to be legalized once more. Gavin delivered a copy of the rules governing his club—based on the Queensberry Rules—to New York senator and future New York City mayor James J. Walker. Walker had a fondness for boxing and the Walker Law legalizing boxing was passed in 1920. Walker also helped organize the sport by instituting licensing of boxers, referees, managers, and promoters under the control of the New York State Athletic Commission (NYAC).

Other states soon passed guidelines similar to the Walker Law. In an attempt to organize a federal body that would control boxing throughout the nation, Gavin established the National Boxing Association (NBA) that same year. Only thirteen states became members, however, limiting the group's authority. The group would remain

Jim Jeffries (left) and Jack Johnson fight in Reno, Nevada, in 1910. Johnson's victory in the championship match sparked rioting throughout the United States.

in existence until 1962 when it became the World Boxing Association (WBA).

The Golden Era of Boxing

The passage of the Walker Law helped pave the way for what would become known as the golden era of boxing. The most famous fighter of this period was Jack Dempsey. He defeated Willard to win the heavyweight title in 1919, and went on to become a boxing legend. Together with his manager Jack "Doc" Kearns and promoter Tex Rickard, Dempsey helped raise the sport to new heights.

Often referred to as simply "the Champ," Dempsey did most of his fighting in Colorado, Utah, and Nevada until hooking up with Kearns. Within a year, Kearns helped mold him into the top contender for the heavyweight championship. Rickard promoted most of Dempsey's fights, including his bout with Georges Carpentier—called "the Battle of the Century"—which produced boxing's first million-dollar gate.

THE RING

In 1922 Nathaniel S. "Nat" Fleischer founded *The Ring* magazine just as boxing was experiencing a surge in popularity. He remained editor and publisher for fifty years, during which time the magazine came to be regarded as "the Bible of Boxing."

Fleischer editorialized on issues facing the sport he loved, including corruption, safety, and the influence of television. In 1925 the magazine began publishing its monthly ratings, listing the top fighters in each weight class. These ratings quickly became accepted as the standard for the sport. Sixteen years later, he issued the first volume of *The Ring Record Book*. From 1941 through 1986–1987, it was regarded as the foremost boxing reference work.

In 1922 Fleischer began presenting The Ring Championship Belt to the undisputed champions in each division. He did so until his death in 1972. At that point, ownership of the magazine passed on to his son-in-law Nat Loubet, who ran the *The Ring* until 1979. The magazine was published under a series of new owners for another decade until financial woes forced it to cease publication in May 1989. Publication resumed in January 1990 and continues to the present day.

(The total receipts of $1,789,238 were nearly four times the previous record.) Four of Dempsey's other matches also surpassed the $1 million mark, including his second fight with Gene Tunney, which set an all-time record of $2,658,660. As Dempsey later said, "My big gates did more to commercialize fighting than anything else in pugilistic history."[15]

The heavyweights were not the only ones drawing interest, however. The 1920s saw the establishment of two new weight classes—junior lightweight (130 pounds) and light welterweight (140 pounds)—and the emergence of many extraordinary fighters in various divisions. Among the best were light heavyweight/middleweight Harry Greb, middleweight/welterweight Mickey Walker, lightweight Benny Leonard, featherweight Tony Canzoneri, bantamweight Panama Al Brown, and flyweight Jimmy Wilde.

Underworld Connections

The 1920s was also the decade of Prohibition. Gangsters across the nation made vast fortunes distributing illegal liquor. Many of these men came from disadvantaged backgrounds where violence was a way of life. It is perhaps natural, therefore, that they took a strong interest in boxing. The chance to make additional money through gambling and fixing fights was an opportunity many could not pass up. By the end of the decade, the mob had become

The referee counts out Jack Sharkey in a match with Primo Carnera. Although many of Carnera's fights were fixed, Sharkey denied taking a fall.

a force to be reckoned with in the world of boxing.

One prime example of the influence wielded by crooks could be seen in the career of Primo Carnera. Carnera was a giant of a man (six feet, six inches tall, 266 pounds) who had been a strongman in a circus in his native Italy. He was introduced to boxing by Leon See, a Frenchman who taught him the basics of the sport. When Carnera came to the United States, he came under the influence of a group connected with racketeer Dutch Schultz and killer Owney Madden.

It is generally accepted that many of Carnera's fights were fixed, with the intent of setting him up for a title match. He eventually got his shot against champion Jack Sharkey in 1933. Despite being outboxed for the first five rounds, Carnera dethroned Sharkey with a sixth-round knockout on a punch that some observers said missed by several inches. Sharkey denied having taken a fall, explaining, "I had no trouble with him in the second bout [he had defeated Carnera in an earlier fight], but all of a sudden—and I can't convince anybody of this, even my own wife has her doubts, I think—I see [Ernie] Schaaf [a protégé of Mr. Sharkey who had died four months earlier after fighting Carnera] in front of me. The next thing I know, I'd lost the championship of the world."[16]

The BBBC

While the underworld was exerting its influence on boxing in the United States, control of the sport in Britain was also undergoing a change. The Boxing Board of Control (BBC) had been formed in 1918 consisting of representatives from various sporting organizations. Since the majority were from the National Sporting Club, however, that association continued to dominate the sport.

With the demise of the original NSC in 1929, the BBC was reorganized as the British Boxing Board of Control (BBBC). It took over control and regulation of boxing (still with a strong NSC influence), including administration of the Lonsdale Belts.

One other group formed during this period was the International Boxing Union (IBU). The purpose of the organization was to regulate the sport on an international basis. Founded in Paris in 1920, the IBU comprised thirteen nations: Argentina, Australia, Brazil, Canada, Denmark, France, Great Britain, Holland, Italy, Norway, Sweden, Switzerland, and the United States. Unfortunately the organization proved to be powerless. The United States did not participate and Great Britain soon withdrew. A lack of an effective international governing body remains one of the biggest problems faced by the sport today.

CHAPTER 3

Into the Modern Era

From the excitement generated by the Roaring Twenties, boxing, like everything else, plunged into the Great Depression. It did not rebound until Joe Louis appeared on the scene to give the country a new hero. Following World War II, the sport received a boost through the magic of television. By the end of the century, closed-circuit television and pay-per-view bouts had made international stars and multimillionaires of men like Muhammad Ali and Mike Tyson.

Tex Rickard's Successor

Tex Rickard had hit on a formula for achieving success in boxing. He discovered talented fighters, signed them to exclusive contracts, and then promoted the championship fights in which they appeared. Many of his successful matches were held at Madison Square Garden, which he had built on Eighth Avenue and 49th Street in Manhattan at a cost of $5.5 million.

After Rickard died in 1929, his recipe for success was followed by Mike Jacobs, a former ticket scalper who had invested in several of Rickard's promotions. In 1933 Jacobs joined sportswriters Damon Runyon, Ed Frayne, and Bill Farnsworth to establish the Twentieth Century Sporting Club (TCSC) to promote boxing. Two years later, Jacobs signed young heavyweight Joe Louis to a contract. His association with Louis cemented his standing as a top boxing promoter.

In 1937 Madison Square Garden leased the arena to the Twentieth Century Sporting Club. Within a year, Jacobs became the sole shareholder of the TCSC and a partner in the Garden. He now had complete control over boxing in New York.

The Brown Bomber

Jacobs's domination of the boxing scene came about primarily through his contract with the Brown Bomber, Joe Louis. Louis rose through the heavyweight ranks to become one of the sport's all-time great fighters. Prior to his ascension to the crown, the heavyweight championship had changed hands five times in six years. After knocking out James J. Braddock to win the title

in 1937, Louis successfully defended his crown twenty-five times over the next eleven years, which included a four-year layoff from 1942 to 1946 when he joined the army during World War II.

Louis brought life back to boxing, becoming the most popular and successful heavyweight champion since Jack Dempsey. With Jacobs promoting his bouts, Louis grossed $4,626,721.69 over the course of his career, a significant amount for that day and age. In his first-round knockout over Max Schmeling in 1938, he collected $349,288.40, or an average of $2,832 per second—a record at the time for a championship fight. Unfortunately Louis lost most of his fortune to

A referee holds up Joe Louis's arm and announces his victory in a match. Louis is one of boxing's all-time great fighters.

bad investments and high living. By the time he hung up his gloves, he owed the Internal Revenue Service over $1 million.

Television Enters the Picture

After his retirement Louis decided to go into business with the International Boxing Club (IBC), an organization formed by Chicago grain millionaire James D. Norris in 1949. Norris signed up many of the leading heavyweight contenders. At Louis's suggestion, the IBC announced that two of them—Ezzard Charles and Jersey Joe Walcott—would meet for Louis's vacated title.

Norris saw the possibilities provided by the new medium of television. He ushered in the era by signing a contract to televise seventy boxing events a year, offering viewers a chance to see some of the top names in the sport. Sponsored by Gillette razor and Pabst Blue Ribbon beer, the shows gave boxing new visibility. The move proved to be the death knell for many small arenas around the country, however. Fans who could see the top fighters each week for free on television were hesitant to pay to see second-rate boxers at local venues. The sport would never be the same.

An Undefeated Champion

The IBC quickly moved to the forefront of the sport. Much of Norris's success was due to his relationships with two of the leading fighters of the day, Sugar Ray Robinson and Rocky Marciano. Robinson held the world welterweight title from 1946 to 1951 and the middleweight crown five times between 1951 and 1960. Many consider him to be the greatest boxer who ever lived.

Marciano was a bruising heavyweight, a man with power, desire, and a solid chin. A crude brawler, Marciano won thirty-eight fights in a row before fighting Louis, who had come out of retirement due to his financial problems. Marciano handed the former champion the third loss of his career, knocking him out in the eighth round of their 1951 battle. As James P. Dawson of *The New York Times* reported, "Fighting before the largest crowd of his career, Rocky proved himself every inch a fighting man. He was crude and awkward so far as ring finesse is concerned, but amazing in his resistance to punishment and altogether destructive in administering it."[17]

The Brockton Blockbuster defended his title six times before retiring in 1955. His place in boxing history is secure as the only heavyweight champion to go undefeated for his professional career. Of his forty-nine bouts, Marciano won forty-three by knockout and six by decision.

The Youngest Champion

A successor to Marciano was found when 1952 Olympic gold medalist Floyd Patterson defeated Tommy "Hurricane" Jackson for the chance to meet light

THE INTERNATIONAL BOXING HALL OF FAME

In 1982 the town of Canastota, New York, decided to honor two of its native sons: Carmen Basilio, world middleweight and welterweight champion of the 1950s, and his nephew, Billy Backus, also a former welterweight titleholder. Residents of the town raised funds to build statues honoring the pair. The success of the drive encouraged the townspeople to expand on their original plan and to establish boxing's first true hall of fame and museum. Since the sport's origin has no ties to a particular geographical area, boxing had never had a "natural" site for a hall of fame as do baseball (Cooperstown, New York), football (Canton, Ohio), and basketball (Springfield, Massachusetts). *The Ring* magazine had established its own Boxing Hall of Fame in 1954, but it was abandoned after 1987.

The International Boxing Hall of Fame opened its doors in 1989, and the first class of inductees was admitted the following year. New members are elected yearly in five categories: Observers, Non-Participants, Pioneers, Old Timers, and Moderns. Things to see at the hall include an exhibit of fist castings of the fighters, a collection of championship belts, and an extensive library.

heavyweight champion Archie Moore for the title. Patterson surprised the favored Moore, recording a fifth-round knockout. By doing so, he became the youngest heavyweight champion of all, claiming the crown at the age of twenty-one years, ten months, and twenty-six days.

After defending his title successfully against Jackson, Pete Rademacher, Roy Harris, and Brian London, Patterson was upset by Sweden's Ingemar Johansson in 1959. Fewer than twenty thousand fans attended the bout at New York's Yankee Stadium, bringing in less than $500,000. Closed-circuit television, however, brought in more than $1 million. For the first time in history, the television revenue accounted for more than the live gate.

The same pattern was repeated in the rematch the following year. Patterson knocked out Johansson in the fifth round to become the first man in history to regain the heavyweight championship. A crowd of over thirty-one thousand at the Polo Grounds in New York brought in $824,814.07. More important, however, were the television, motion picture, and radio rights. With the fight televised to 230 closed-circuit locations in 160 cities, the final financial figures approximated $2.5 million.

The IBC and Organized Crime

For more than a decade, the IBC had been the primary force behind boxing in the United States. After staging the championship fight between Ezzard Charles and Jersey Joe Walcott in 1949, the IBC bought out Mike Jacobs's Twentieth Century Sporting Club and became affiliated with Madison Square Garden in New York City. The organization promoted nearly every championship fight in every division, giving it a virtual monopoly over the sport.

In 1958 the U.S. Supreme Court ordered the group's breakup for violating the Sherman Anti-Trust Act due to "conspiracy to control the promotion of world championship fights throughout the USA."[18] When U.S. senator Estes Kefauver led an investigation into underworld involvement in the sport, he found that mobster Frankie Carbo was the real power behind the group. If a fighter or manager refused to go along with the IBC, he was blackballed, or prevented from getting meaningful fights.

Boxers came forward with damaging testimony. Former middleweight champion Jake LaMotta, for example, testified that he threw a 1947 fight with Billy Fox. He agreed to the arrangement in order to get a future chance at the championship. "I thought it was right then," he said. "I just wanted to be champion."[19]

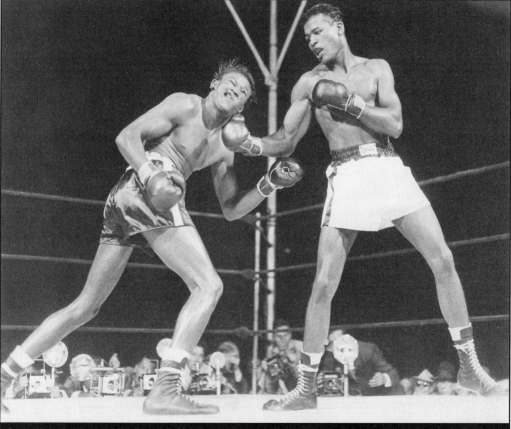

Sugar Ray Robinson (right) punches Kid Gavilan in a 1948 match. Many fans consider Robinson to be the greatest boxer who ever lived.

In the end Carbo was convicted of conspiracy and extortion for trying to muscle in on the earnings of former welterweight champion Don Jordan. He was sentenced to twenty-five years in prison, causing Attorney General Robert F. Kennedy to say, "Frank Carbo has been a sinister figure behind the scenes in boxing for more than twenty years. This verdict will be a great aid and assistance to the Department of Justice and local law enforcement authorities in taking further action against the attempts of racketeers to control boxing and other sports."[20]

The Beginning of an Era

Although Carbo was out of the picture, his underworld influence could still be seen in the career of Sonny Liston, who ended Patterson's second reign as heavyweight champion in 1962. Liston was a shadowy figure with a police record. His career had been guided by Frank "Blinky" Palermo, another underworld figure who had been convicted on conspiracy and extortion charges along with Carbo. Liston wrested the title from Patterson with a first-round knockout and then repeated the feat eight months later in the rematch.

Although Liston's two quick knockouts made him appear invincible to many, he came crashing to earth in his very next fight. His opponent was a brash young man from Louisville, Kentucky, named Cassius Marcellus Clay. Clay would soon change his name to Muhammad Ali and become the most recognized athlete in the world, known to one and all by his self-proclaimed nickname, "the Greatest."

Ali was a master showman who infuriated opponents and fans with his brash ranting while amazing them with his fists. In the first part of his pro career, he earned a reputation as a loudmouthed braggart, entertaining the media with his poems, predictions, and antics outside of the ring. He was stripped of his title when he refused induction into the armed forces, but he eventually won the fans over to become one of the best-loved athletes of the twentieth century. Ali had a flashy, distinctive style, highlighted by unbelievable hand and foot speed that helped him avoid opponents' punches. (Author Norman Mailer once said of Ali, "He worked apparently on the premise that there was something obscene about being hit."[21]) Ali became the first boxer in history to win the heavyweight title three times.

Confusion in the Heavyweight Ranks

When Ali refused induction into the army in 1967, both the World Boxing Association (WBA) and World Boxing Council (WBC) stripped him of his title. The WBA had been formed in 1962, succeeding the NBA, which had been a force in boxing since 1927. It originally consisted of most of the city and state boxing commissions

Muhammad Ali raises his arms in victory after knocking out his opponent. Ali was the first boxer in history to win the heavyweight title three times.

and federations outside of New York. In 1963 the WBC was founded to counter the WBA's claims of authority. The WBC was comprised of the BBBC, the European Boxing Union (EBU), and authorities from several other nations. It also had the support of the NYAC. The result was that the WBA and WBC had effectively replaced the NBA and NYAC as the two main boxing organizations. This new reorganization of power set the stage for disagreements over world champions that have continued up through the present day.

The WBA moved to find a successor to Ali by staging an eight-man tournament comprising Oscar Bonavena, Jimmy Ellis,

Joe Frazier, Karl Mildenberger, Floyd Patterson, Jerry Quarry, Thad Spencer, and Ernie Terrell. (When Frazier refused to join the group, he was replaced by Leotis Martin.) Ellis emerged as the victor to become the WBA champion. Frazier, in the meantime, defeated Buster Mathis to become the WBC titleholder. The two champs eventually met in 1970. Frazier came out on top to become the undisputed champion.

King of the Promoters

Over the next decade, the heavyweight division was dominated by Joe Frazier, George Foreman, Muhammad Ali, and Larry Holmes. Many of the most famous—and most successful—fights of this period were promoted by Don King.

King was a former numbers runner who turned his life around after serving time in prison for manslaughter. He got

WOMEN'S BOXING

Women's boxing can be traced all the way back to early-eighteenth-century London. Not until 1876, however, was the first such match held in the United States. Women's boxing was a displayed event (a demonstration rather than a competition for a medal) in the 1904 Olympics held in St. Louis. Aside from occasional exhibitions, however, the sport did not really begin to catch on until the mid-1970s.

In 1975 Caroline Svendsen became the first woman to receive a boxing license in the United States, doing so in Nevada. Over the next few years, other states followed Nevada's example. Some of the higher profile women boxers of this period were Pat Pineda, Cathy "Cat" Davis, Jackie Tonawanda, and Marian "Lady Tyger" Trimiar.

March 15, 1996, is considered by many to be the birth of women's professional boxing. A worldwide audience watched Christy Martin and Deirdre Gogarty stage a bloody six-round brawl as one of the fights on the undercard of the Mike Tyson–Frank Bruno pay-per-view event. Martin became the subject of a cover story in *Sports Illustrated* magazine several weeks later.

Muhammad Ali's daughter Laila Ali throws a punch at Jacqui Frazier-Lyde in 2001.

The modern-day fighter who has done the most to bring attention to women's boxing is Laila Ali, daughter of former world heavyweight champion Muhammad Ali. On June 8, 2001, Ali fought Jacqui Frazier-Lyde, daughter of her father's longtime rival Joe Frazier. The eight-round match won by Ali drew an impressive one hundred thousand pay-per-view buys.

into the promotional end of the sport, with his first major coup being the Muhammad Ali–George Foreman "Rumble in the Jungle" in Zaire in 1974. Each of the two fighters received $5 million for the fight, an unheard-of sum at the time.

Since then, King has promoted more than five hundred championship fights. He has earned millions of dollars for the boxers he signed and even more for himself. In his three decades in boxing, King has often been accused of stealing money from the boxers he represented. Among other things, he has also been investigated by the FBI and questioned by Congress about payoffs, possible racketeering, and an alleged association with underworld figures, and he has been accused of income tax and insurance fraud. Despite all this, the flamboyant King has generally managed to stay one step ahead of the law and maintain his position as arguably the most powerful man in boxing.

In 1986 King, together with the Home Box Office (HBO) cable television network, set up a series of fights with the intention of unifying the world heavyweight championship. The matches would pair off the three titleholders—the WBA, WBC, and International Boxing Federation (IBF), a new organization that came into existence in 1983—and the leading heavyweight contenders.

The climax of the series took place on August 1, 1987, in Las Vegas, Nevada.

There a young fighter from Brooklyn, New York, defeated Tony Tucker to become the undisputed heavyweight champion of the world. That boxer— Mike Tyson—would become one of the most controversial figures in the history of the sport.

The Seeds of Greatness

Tyson made the journey from the streets of Brownsville to the heavyweight championship of the world in record time. He came to the attention of famed trainer Cus D'Amato at a young age. He learned his lessons well and turned professional in 1985. Tyson finished his first year as a pro with a record of 15-0 with fifteen knockouts. On November 26, 1986, he knocked out Trevor Berbick to win the WBC title at the tender age of twenty years and five months to become the youngest heavyweight champion ever.

Tyson claimed the WBA crown with a victory over James "Bonecrusher" Smith in March 1987 and then proceeded to become the unified champion with his knockout of Tucker less than five months later. Tyson defended his title against all comers and entered 1990 with a record of 37-0 with thirty-three knockouts. Most of his bouts did not last long. Included was a ninety-one-second victory over former undefeated champ Michael Spinks for which Tyson received an unprecedented $20 million.

Mike Tyson (right) pummels Francois Botha in a 1999 match. Tyson is one of the most controversial figures in boxing.

On February 11, 1990, however, 42-1 underdog Buster Douglas knocked out Tyson in perhaps the greatest upset in sports history. By that time, Tyson's personal life had started to unravel. His brief marriage to actress Robin Givens ended in divorce, and he was taking medication to treat depression. He crashed several cars and was involved in fights outside of the ring. In July 1991 he allegedly sexually assaulted Miss Black America contestant Desiree Washington. He was charged with rape, found guilty, and sentenced to six years in prison.

Out of Control

Tyson returned to the ring following his release in March 1995 after serving three years. He defeated Peter McNeeley in just one round in his first fight after nearly four years of inactivity. One year later, he became the third fighter to regain the heavyweight crown, winning the WBC title with a third-round knockout of Frank Bruno. In a much-anticipated match eight months later, Tyson was defeated by Evander Holyfield for the WBA title.

From that point on, Tyson was involved in one bizarre incident after another. In a rematch with Holyfield in June 1997, he

THE 1976 U.S. OLYMPIC DREAM TEAM

The 1976 U.S. Olympic boxing team that competed in Montreal, Canada, is often referred to as the Dream Team. Although they were not the most prolific medal winners, their victories were significant in that four of the five came against the reigning Olympic superpowers, Cuba and the Soviet Union.

The first American to win gold was flyweight Lee Randolph, who defeated Cuba's Ramon Duvalon. Lightweight Howard Davis followed with a victory over Romania's Simion Cutov. Brothers Leon and Michael Spinks became the first siblings to take Olympic boxing titles by winning the light heavyweight and middleweight gold medals, respectively. The fifth American to emerge victorious was Sugar Ray Leonard, who won in the light welterweight division.

The Americans were successful in their future professional careers as well. Leonard went on to become one of boxing's great champions, the first man to win belts in five weight divisions. Leon Spinks upset Muhammad Ali for the heavyweight crown in 1978. Brother Michael won both the light heavyweight championship and a share of the heavyweight title. Randolph, the youngest of the five, became WBA junior featherweight champ in 1980.

Davis was the only one of the gold medalists who did not win a pro belt, losing all four of his title shots. Another member of the 1976 team, however, did add a pro crown. Heavyweight John Tate, who won a bronze medal in Montreal, had a brief term as WBA heavyweight champ in 1979.

Leon (left) and Michael Spinks are the first brothers to win Olympic boxing titles.

was disqualified after the third round for biting off a piece of Holyfield's ear in retaliation for a head butt that opened a gash over his eye. His license was revoked by the Nevada State Athletic Commission, which fined him $3 million for the incident. The following March, he filed a $100-million lawsuit against promoter Don King, accusing King of cheating him out of millions of dollars. In February 1999 Tyson was again sent to prison, this time for assaulting two motorists.

Upon his release, Tyson again returned to the ring. In June 2000 he stopped Lou Savarese in just thirty-eight seconds of their bout in Scotland and then knocked down the referee in order to keep hitting Savarese after the fight was stopped. While the BBBC waited to discuss possible sanctions against him, Tyson announced that he was ready for a title shot against champion Lennox Lewis. Proclaimed Tyson, "When I'm ready I'm going to rip out his heart and feed it to him. My style is impetuous, my defense is impregnable and I'm just ferocious. I want your heart. I want to eat your children. Praise be to Allah."[22] Unfortunately for Tyson, Lewis was even more ferocious. When they finally met on June 8, 2002, Tyson was knocked out in the eighth round.

To some people, Mike Tyson is symbolic of what boxing has become today: controversial, out of control, and past its peak. Although many are sounding boxing's death knell, there are just as many who continue to be fervent fans, optimistic about the sport's future. To those, boxing remains the ultimate sporting event: two men fighting one another, using only their fists, in the oldest, most basic form of competition of all.

CHAPTER 4

The Gladiators

As novelist and boxing enthusiast Joyće Carol Oates wrote in her 1987 book *On Boxing*, "An ambitious boxer in our times hopes not only to be a champion but to be a great champion—an immortal."[23] Only a small fraction of the thousands of men who have fought professionally have attained such exalted status. Their successes have made them household names, not just in this country but around the world.

Jack Johnson

Jack Johnson was one of the most controversial figures in a controversial sport. He was one of the greatest heavyweight champions of all time but also one of the most hated. The latter was tied to the fact

that he was the first African American heavyweight champ.

Born in Galveston, Texas, in 1878, Johnson was the son of a former slave. He honed his boxing skills in local battle royals. Johnson turned professional at the age of nineteen in 1897. He won the black heavyweight title six years later but was denied a shot at the world title because of his race. He finally got his chance in 1908 when he faced champion Tommy Burns in Australia. Aware of the prejudice he faced, Johnson predicted, "For every point I'm given, I'll have earned two, because I'm a negro."[24] Not taking any chances, he pummeled his foe, causing the bout to be stopped in the fourteenth round with Johnson emerging as the new champion.

The sporting community immediately set out to find a "Great White Hope" who could wrest the title from Johnson. The champion, however, soundly thrashed all comers. On July 4, 1910, he defeated former heavyweight champ Jim Jeffries in the first "Fight of the Century." Johnson received an incredible $117,000 for his day's work.

Johnson enraged white society outside of the ring with his flamboyant lifestyle. His interracial romances were especially galling to racists of the day. Johnson was eventually convicted of transporting a minor across state lines for immoral purposes, a violation of the Mann Act, the so-called white slavery act. Even though the teenaged white woman was his wife, he was sentenced to a year in prison and fined $1,000. Before he could be incarcerated, Johnson fled the country and spent the next seven years on the run.

Johnson continued to fight overseas and eventually lost a controversial match to Jess Willard in Havana, Cuba, in 1915. He was knocked out in the twenty-sixth round, but rumors persisted that he threw the fight. (In a famous photograph, he is shown on his back after the knockdown, apparently shading his eyes from

The son of a former slave, Jack Johnson faced tremendous prejudice as the first African American heavyweight champ.

the sun—an unlikely action for someone dazed and tired after twenty-six rounds of boxing.) Johnson later claimed that he was indeed paid to throw the match.

Johnson returned to the United States in 1920. He surrendered to the authorities and served eight months in Leavenworth prison in Kansas. Following his release, he fought several more times before finally retiring at the age of fifty. Johnson was killed in an automobile accident in 1946. Eight years later, he became one of the charter members of the Boxing Hall of Fame.

Jack Dempsey

William Harrison "Jack" Dempsey was one of America's first great sports heroes. He captured the imagination of the sporting public with his savage style and raw power. "In the ring," wrote Pulitzer Prize–winning sportswriter Red Smith, "he was a tiger without mercy who shuffled forward in a bobbing crouch, humming a barely audible tune and punching to the rhythm of the song. He was 187 pounds of unbridled violence."[25]

Born in 1895, Dempsey was one of eleven children raised in poverty in Manassa, Colorado. He set out on his own after graduating from the eighth grade. Dempsey worked as an itinerant laborer and fought in local clubs whenever he could. In 1917 he was recruited by veteran manager Jack "Doc" Kearns. Within

a year and a half, Dempsey was matched against Jess Willard for the heavyweight title. The Manassa Mauler, as he came to be known, defeated the much bigger champion, administering a terrific beating in the process in their 1919 bout.

Dempsey's aggressive style made him a popular attraction among ring fans. They came out in droves to see the raw power that produced forty-nine knockouts in a seventy-eight-bout career, including twenty-five in the first round. Dempsey defended his heavyweight title against Georges Carpentier in 1921, which generated boxing's first $1-million gate. Six years later, he faced Gene Tunney in the sport's first $2-million gate.

Despite his prowess in the ring, Dempsey was not a fan favorite. During World War I, he had been charged with draft evasion, and although a jury exonerated him of the charge, many members of the sporting public still held it against him. It was not until he lost the championship and fought Gene Tunney in the famous "Long Count" rematch that he became more popular with the fans.

Dempsey retired shortly after the Tunney fight, although he continued to fight exhibition bouts over the next few years. During World War II, he served as a director of the Coast Guard physical fitness program and as a morale officer in the Pacific. His patriotic activities helped increase his popularity. Following the war,

Dempsey returned to New York City where he operated a popular restaurant. In 1950 he was named the greatest fighter of the first half-century in an Associated Press poll.

Henry Armstrong

Henry Armstrong will always be remembered by ring fans as the only man to hold three world titles simultaneously. Making the feat even more extraordinary was the fact that he did so at a time when there were only eight weight classes, not the inflated number that exists nowadays.

Born Henry Jackson on December 12, 1912, Armstrong began boxing under the name Melody Jackson. He was knocked out in his first pro fight in 1931 at the age of eighteen. He resumed fighting as an amateur by taking the surname of his trainer, Henry Armstrong. After failing to make the 1932 Olympic team, Armstrong again turned pro as a featherweight. After winning a 1936 bout against Baby Arizmendi, his contract was purchased by legendary jazz singer Al Jolson, who had witnessed the fight. Eddie Mead, who became Armstrong's manager, guided him to his first title.

In that match, Armstrong won the featherweight crown by knocking out champion Petey Sarron on October 29, 1937. Seven months later, he won a unanimous fifteen-round decision over Barney Ross to take the welterweight title. He added the lightweight crown to his collection less than three months after that by earning a split decision in a hard-fought battle with Lou Amber. Armstrong was severely cut during the bout and warned by referee Billy Cavanaugh that the contest would be stopped if he spit out any more blood. Armstrong had his cornermen remove his mouthpiece between rounds so that he could swallow the blood flowing from his mouth. He did this for the last five rounds on his way to victory. After the fight the cut in his mouth required thirty-seven stitches.

Armstrong attempted to become the first-ever four-division champion when he took on Ceferino Garcia for the middleweight crown in 1940. In another hard-fought match, however, Garcia retained the crown by gaining a draw. Armstrong's greatness in the ring was attested to by Fritzie Zivic, who took the welterweight crown from him in 1940. "Hank," said Zivic, "you're the greatest champ that ever walked."[26]

Archie Moore

Born in Benoit, Mississippi, on December 13, 1913, Archibald Lee Wright—better known as Archie Moore—had one of the longest, most successful careers in the history of professional boxing. He made his pro debut in 1936 and did not hang up his gloves until twenty-seven years later at the age of fifty. He retired with a record of

RUBIN CARTER

Although never a world champion, Rubin "Hurricane" Carter was one of the hardest punchers of the 1960s. More than as a boxer, however, Carter has become a symbol of courage whose story was told in the full-length motion picture *The Hurricane* starring Denzel Washington.

Carter turned professional in 1961 and quickly fought his way up through the middleweight ranks. He finally got a title shot against champion Joey Giardello in 1964, losing a close decision. Two years later, his world came crashing down around him.

On June 17, 1966, two men and a woman were fatally shot in a New Jersey bar and grill. Carter and John Artis were arrested and charged with the crime. Despite passing lie-detector tests, both men were convicted, based on the testimony of two convicted felons. The two black defendants were sentenced by an all-white jury to three life sentences.

By 1974 the two main witnesses who had placed Carter and Artis at the scene recanted their stories, saying they had been pressured by the authorities to lie. The case gained national attention, and the two men finally had their convictions overturned. A second trial in 1976, however, found them guilty once again. (The two witnesses again changed their stories.) Finally, in 1985, federal district judge H. Lee Sarokin released Carter and Artis on the grounds that the convictions "were predicated on an appeal to racism rather than reason, and concealment rather than disclosure." Two years later, twenty-two years after the murders, the original indictments against the men were dismissed for good. Today, Rubin Carter heads the Association in Defence of the Wrongly Convicted in Toronto, Canada.

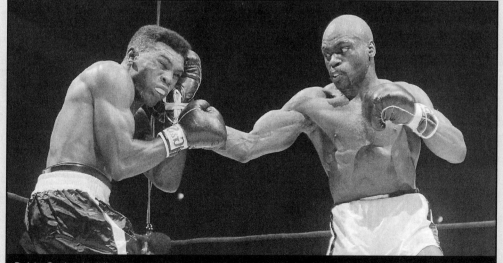

Rubin Carter (right) was wrongfully convicted of murder and he served nineteen years in prison before an appellate judge overturned his conviction.

Henry Armstrong accepts the world welterweight championship trophy in 1939. Armstrong is the only boxer to hold three world titles simultaneously.

194-26 with eight draws. He is generally credited with 145 knockouts for the all-time mark, although some sources put the figure at 141.

Known as "the Old Mongoose" (because of his cleverness and trickery, like a mongoose that can kill venomous snakes), Moore started out as a middleweight and then moved up to the light heavyweight division in the mid-1940s. Despite beating most of the top contenders of the day, he failed to get a shot at the title until 1952 when he won the crown with a unanimous decision over Joey Maxim at the advanced age of thirty-nine. He successfully defended the title nine times over the next decade.

Moore decided to step up a class in weight in 1955 in order to try to wrest the heavyweight crown from Rocky Marciano. Moore dropped the undefeated champion in the second round, but the much younger Marciano bounced back to knock Moore down three times. When the referee offered to stop the fight after the eighth round, Moore turned the offer down, replying, "I too am a champion, and I want to go out like a champion."[27] Marciano continued his assault and finally stopped Moore in the next round.

Moore got another shot at the heavyweight crown after Marciano retired. He fought Floyd Patterson for the vacated title but was knocked out in the fifth round. Patterson, at twenty, was less than half Moore's age.

One of Moore's most famous fights was his 1958 title defense against Yvon Durelle. The powerful Canadian dropped Moore twice in the opening round and once more in round five. The veteran hung on, however, to knock Durelle down in the tenth before finishing him off in round eleven. Many veteran observers consider the bout one of the greatest of all time.

Moore was eventually stripped of his light heavyweight crown in 1962 when he decided to fight solely as a heavyweight. In his last major fight, he was knocked out in four rounds by future heavyweight champ Cassius Clay (Muhammad Ali). He fought one last time, knocking out Mike DiBiase in three rounds in 1963. Moore was selected as one of the original members of the International Boxing Hall of Fame in 1990.

Joe Louis

When veteran ring observers rank the greatest heavyweights of all time, Joe Louis's name always appears near the top of the list. His record of twenty-five successful title defenses has never been matched in the heavyweight division. Even more important than his victories in the

---

PETE RADEMACHER

When Thomas Peter Rademacher stepped into the ring at Sicks' Stadium in Seattle on August 22, 1957, he made boxing history. He became the only man to fight for the heavyweight title in his first professional match. A 10-1 underdog, Rademacher had champion Floyd Patterson on the canvas one time before being knocked out himself in round six.

As an amateur, Rademacher had represented the United States ten months prior to that in the 1956 Olympic Games in Melbourne, Australia. Earlier that year, Russian troops had invaded Hungary. When Rademacher stopped Russian Lev Moukhine for the gold medal, the members of the Hungarian team stormed the ring and lifted him up on their shoulders. As Rademacher later recalled in Angelo Bruscas's article "Rademacher, 72, Still in There Swinging for Olympic Ideal," "It was the free world versus Russia. I kind of think I helped end the Cold War in the Olympic village that night."

After his defeat at the hands of Patterson, Rademacher proceeded to forge a lackluster 17-6-1 record as a pro. Following his retirement, he entered the business world. He joined Kiefer McNeil of Akron, Ohio, in 1965 and became president of the company nine years later. Rademacher has helped develop several patented products, including a shotgun device that trains people to shoot with both eyes open, kickboards and leg-floating devices used in competitive swimming, a swimming pool chlorinator, wave-quelling line dividers (which lessen the effects of waves produced by swimmers during races), and a motorized unicycle.

ring, however, was his role as a model for blacks everywhere. He was the first African American athlete to be loved and admired by both blacks and whites alike.

Louis was born Joseph Louis Barrow in Lafayette, Alabama, on May 13, 1914, and began taking boxing lessons as a teenager. In his first amateur bout, he was knocked down seven times by U.S. Olympic boxer John Miler. He was not discouraged, however, and came back to win his next match on a first-round knockout.

Louis fought fifty-eight times before turning professional. Under the direction of a Detroit entrepreneur named John Roxborough, he began to climb up through the heavyweight ranks, defeating former champions Primo Carnera and Max Baer in the process. The Brown Bomber won his first twenty-seven pro fights—twenty-three by knockout—before suffering his first defeat at the hands of former champion Max Schmeling. He bounced back from the loss and won the heavyweight title from James J. Braddock on June 22, 1937. Exactly one year later, Louis exacted his revenge on Schmeling, handing the German a terrific beating. The match was popularly viewed as a victory for democracy over Nazism since Schmeling was Adolf Hitler's designated example of Aryan superiority.

Louis defended his title a total of twenty-five times over an eleven-year period, which included a four-year stretch in the service. He took on all comers, many of whom were referred to, collectively, as the Bum-of-the-Month Club. Two of Louis's most memorable fights were with light heavyweight champion Billy Conn. In the first, in June 1941, Conn was ahead on all scorecards until Louis knocked him out in the thirteenth round. In the rematch—after Louis returned from the service—the champ retained his crown with a knockout in round eight.

With age catching up to him, Louis retired on March 1, 1949. Strapped for cash, however, he was forced to make a comeback the following year. He lost a fifteen-round decision to champion Ezzard Charles and then fought several more times before being knocked out in his final appearance by future champion Rocky Marciano in 1951.

Louis retired with a record of sixty-two wins and three losses. Forty-nine of his wins were by knockout. He is a member of the International Boxing Hall of Fame and had a sports complex—the Joe Louis Arena—named after him in Detroit. Louis will always be remembered as a winner and a champion who helped bring people of all races together. As legendary sports columnist Jimmy Cannon once wrote, "His people say he was a credit to his race. They sell him short. He was a credit to the human race."[28]

Joe Louis defended his heavyweight title twenty-five times, a boxing record that still stands.

Sugar Ray Robinson

Sugar Ray Robinson is recognized by many historians as, pound-for-pound, the best boxer who ever lived. Born Walker Smith Jr. in 1921, he was sparring in a Harlem gym when he borrowed the Amateur Athletic Union (AAU) card of a friend named Ray Robinson. When manager George Gainford noticed Smith's

potential to be a fine boxer he mentioned that he was "sweet as sugar,"[29] and the name Sugar Ray Robinson was born.

Robinson made a name for himself by winning the New York Golden Gloves title. He turned pro at age nineteen and advanced through the ranks, defeating Tommy Bell for the vacant welterweight championship in late 1946. Robinson dominated the division, going ninety-one consecutive fights without a loss. He finally suffered a stunning defeat at the hands of Randy Turpin in 1951 but regained the crown in a rematch two months later. Earlier that year, Robinson had won the middleweight title from Jake LaMotta in a brawl remembered as the St. Valentine Day Massacre because Robinson administered a terrific beating to LaMotta. It was the sixth—and final—time the two future Hall of Famers met in the ring, with Robinson winning five of the matchups.

Over the next nine years, Robinson won the middleweight crown four more times, doing so with victories over Randy Turpin, Carl "Bobo" Olson, Gene Fullmer, and Carmen Basilio. In June 1952 he fought

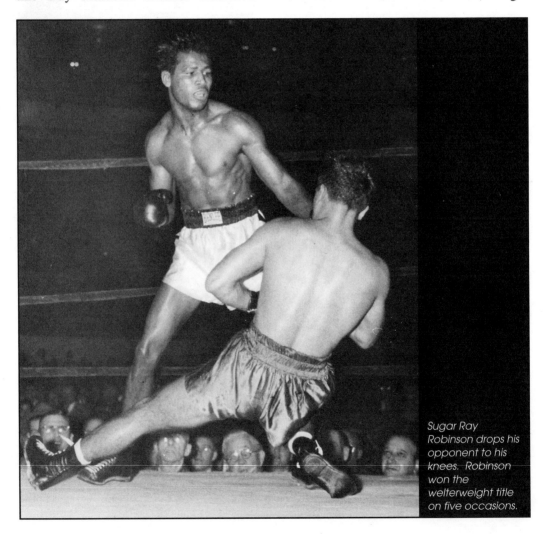

Sugar Ray Robinson drops his opponent to his knees. Robinson won the welterweight title on five occasions.

Joey Maxim for the light heavyweight championship. Despite being ahead on all three officials' cards, he lost the match when the 103-degree temperature at Yankee Stadium forced him to quit after thirteen rounds. Robinson retired six months later but returned to the ring in 1955. He retired for good in 1965 at the age of forty-four.

Robinson was one of the first black athletes to make a name for himself outside of sports as well as in the ring. He was a popular figure on the New York scene in the forties and fifties with a pink Cadillac convertible, a nightclub in Harlem, and an entourage that followed him everywhere he went.

Robinson hung up his gloves with a career record of 175-19-6 and two no-decisions. His artistry in the ring has perhaps never been matched. As sportswriter Barney Nagler wrote, "He boxed as though he were playing the violin."[30]

Muhammad Ali

Muhammad Ali's self-proclaimed nickname is "the Greatest," and to many people that is exactly what he is—the greatest heavyweight fighter who ever lived. He is the first man to win the title three times, in the process introducing his own distinct style to the sweet science.

Ali entered the world as Cassius Marcellus Clay on January 18, 1942, in Louisville, Kentucky. Clay began fighting at the age of twelve. He won a pair of national Golden Gloves titles as a middleweight, and an Amateur Athletic Union (AAU) championship as a light heavyweight. He made the 1960 U.S. Olympic team and won a gold medal in the light heavyweight competition in Rome. Clay turned professional shortly after returning home.

Clay combined blindingly fast hand and foot speed with a talent for self-promotion to quickly rise through the heavyweight ranks. He bragged that he was the greatest fighter in the world, and also the prettiest. He began to spout poems in which he predicted the round in which his opponent would fall.

On February 25, 1964, Clay shocked the boxing world when he defeated heavily favored champion Sonny Liston for the heavyweight title. The following day, he announced that he had become a Muslim and was changing his name to Muhammad Ali. The move alienated him from much of the white community, many of whom considered Islam an anti-American religion.

After defending his title eight times, Ali's popularity dropped even further in 1967 when he refused to be inducted into the army during the Vietnam War. He sought conscientious objector status on religious grounds and announced, "I ain't got no quarrel with them Viet Cong."[31] He was arrested and had his boxing license suspended. He was also stripped of his heavyweight crown.

TEOFILO STEVENSON

Some people refer to Teofilo Stevenson as "the Cuban Ali." He is one of the greatest heavyweight fighters ever to have put on a pair of gloves, and he is a legend in his native land of Cuba. Born in the small coastal town of Puerto Padre in 1952, Stevenson took up boxing at the age of thirteen. A year later, he was the Cuban junior national champion. When he was just nineteen, the six-foot, four-inch youngster represented Cuba in the 1972 Munich Olympics. Using an accurate left jab and a powerful right hand, he returned home with the gold medal and then repeated his success in Montreal in 1976 and in Moscow in 1980. Stevenson missed a chance for a fourth consecutive gold medal when Cuba boycotted the 1984 games held in Los Angeles.

Following his Olympic victory in 1972, Stevenson was offered $1 million to defect to the United States and turn professional. Staying true to his homeland and Cuban dictator Fidel Castro, however, he refused. He is quoted in Eugene Robinson's article "The Cuban Ali" as saying "What is a million dollars compared to the love of my people?"

Stevenson's boxing career was ended by a near-fatal accident in which a stove in his home exploded. Currently, he is the vice president of the Cuban Boxing Federation.

Ali was sentenced to five years in prison. Released on appeal, his conviction was eventually overturned three years later. He returned to the ring in 1970 and signed to fight undefeated Joe Frazier in what was billed as "the Fight of the Century." In a battle that lived up to the hype, Ali lost to Frazier, suffering his first defeat as a pro.

Ali became the first heavyweight to regain the title by upsetting George Foreman in 1974. He introduced his Rope-A-Dope in the fight, a maneuver in which he allowed Foreman to flail away at his covered-up body while he stood with his back up against the ropes. When the champion tired late in the fight, Ali finished him off.

Ali fought—and defeated—Frazier two more times, including the famous "Thrilla in Manila" in 1975. He lost his crown to Leon Spinks in 1978 and then regained it seven months later. Ali announced his retirement that June but put the gloves back on in 1980 for two last fights, both of which he lost. He retired for good with a record of 56-5.

Years of fighting took their toll on Ali, who developed pugilistic parkinsonism from repetitive trauma to the head. Although this has slowed him down considerably, he still remains active, making numerous appearances at fund-raisers across the country.

CHAPTER 5

The Spectacles

In her book *On Boxing* Joyce Carol Oates says, "Each boxing match is a story—a unique and highly condensed drama without words."[32] The history of the sport is a chronicle of these tales, each with its own story line involving two main characters (the boxers themselves) and several secondary ones (the referee, managers, promoter, and so on). Just as every story is unique, so too is every fight. Some of the more famous matches—such as the 1938 Louis-Schmeling bout—have had an effect extending far beyond the ring itself.

1860 Tom Sayers –John Heenan

The 1860 match between American champion John C. Heenan and British champ Tom Sayers was the first international championship contest. Since prizefighting was still illegal, the bout was held in a meadow in Farnsborough Common, some twenty-five miles outside of London. It spurred interest on both sides of the Atlantic Ocean and drew a large crowd. As Newbold wrote in his *Great Battle for the Championship:*

> The crowd was the most representative ever seen at a fight in our country. Compared to former mills, the present congregation must unhesitatingly be pronounced the most aristocratic ever assembled at a ringside. It included the bearers of names highly distinguished in British society, officers of the Army and navy, of Parliament, justices of the

peace and even brethren of the cloth. The muster of literati included William Thackeray and Charles Dickens.[33]

The six-foot, two-inch, 195-pound Heenan was six inches taller and forty-three pounds heavier than his opponent (who would have been only a middleweight by modern standards). The smaller Sayers, however, had more ring experience. Heenan did most of the damage in the early rounds, breaking the Englishman's right arm with one of his punches in the sixth. Sayers countered by attacking Heenan's face and proceeded to partially shut one of his eyes

in the seventh. The fight continued in this manner for thirty-six rounds, with Heenan using his size advantage to repeatedly throw his opponent to the ground. Sayers parried by regularly hitting the American in the face.

With Sayers showing signs of tiring in the thirty-seventh round, Heenan rushed forward and pinned him with his neck against the top rope. Sensing that Sayers was in danger of being strangled, the unruly partisan crowd cut the rope and surged forward. Perceiving the danger, the referee abandoned the scene, but the two fighters continued to battle for five more

American John Heenan and Britain Tom Sayers fight outside London in 1860. The match was the first international championship contest.

rounds. After forty-two rounds, the police finally intervened. Heenan wanted a new site found to continue the fray, but the fight was ruled a draw, and a championship belt was awarded to each man.

1892 John L. Sullivan– James Corbett

After defending his heavyweight title with a win over Jake Kilrain in 1889, John L. Sullivan decided to take up acting and put his boxing career on hold. He traveled the world on a barnstorming tour in a production of a melodrama called "Honest Hearts and Willing Hands." By 1891 he was being roundly criticized for his lack of pugilistic activity. Tired of the criticism, Sullivan announced he would fight any contender for a winner-take-all purse of $25,000. The only stipulation was that each man had to additionally put up a side bet of $10,000 so that the winner would walk away with $35,000. James J. Corbett raised the funds, and the fight was set for September 7, 1892, in New Orleans, Louisiana, as part of a three-day "Carnival of Champions."

At that time, boxing was still illegal in many places. New Orleans had passed legislation to legalize it in 1890 but only if the bouts were held under the Queensberry Rules, which required the fighters to wear gloves. The Sullivan-Corbett match became the first heavyweight title bout fought under those conditions.

The carnival began on September 5 with a lightweight championship bout between Jack MacAuliffe and Billy Myer. It continued the next day with the featherweight clash between George Dixon and Jack Skelly. The main event between Sullivan and Corbett on September 7 was witnessed by approximately ten thousand fans—at the time the largest crowd ever to attend a fight.

The thirty-three-year-old champion weighed in at 212 pounds for the match while the younger challenger, Corbett, came in 25 pounds lighter. Nevertheless, the elusive Corbett dominated the action, easily avoiding the clumsy rushes of the charging Sullivan. With the champion tiring badly, Corbett sent him to the canvas in the twenty-first round. Sullivan was counted out, Corbett became champion, and a new era had begun.

The fight was Sullivan's last. Addressing the crowd after the bout, he announced, "Gentlemen, gentlemen. I have nothing at all to say. All I have to say is that I came into the ring once too often—and if I had to get licked, I'm glad I was licked by an American. I remain your warm and personal friend, John L. Sullivan."[34]

1923 Jack Dempsey –Luis Firpo

The 1923 heavyweight championship fight between champion Jack Dempsey and challenger Luis Firpo lasted less than four

CHAMPIONSHIP BELTS

With the proliferation of weight classes and boxing organizations, championship belts are more common nowadays than at any time in the past. The first such belt was awarded to bare-knuckle champion Tom Cribb by King George III in 1811. It was constructed of lionskin and sterling silver.

The practice of giving out championship belts in the United States began in the late 1880s by Richard Fox, publisher of the *Police Gazette*, the "official" source of boxing (by Fox's own declaration). Other belts were presented to fighters by their fans, including an $8,000 gold version, adorned with 397 diamonds, that was given to John L. Sullivan by the citizens of his hometown of Boston. (Fox had reportedly once been insulted by Sullivan. Because of this, he had awarded his "official" belt to Jake Kilrain.)

In 1926 *The Ring* magazine began presenting belts to those it recognized as champions. Today, championship belts are awarded by the different boxing organizations, as well as various state commissions. Although the cash value of the modern belts is not what it used to be, the value is high among collectors of sports memorabilia. In 1991 a belt presented to Joe Louis brought $100,000 at auction.

Firpo was a 3-1 underdog. When the bell rang for round one on September 14 in the Polo Grounds in New York City, Dempsey charged from his corner, intent on bringing the fight to a quick conclusion. The crowd of eighty-two thousand looked on as he began his assault. After being caught with a hard left hook, however, Firpo connected with a powerful right of his own, sending the champion to the canvas. Dempsey immediately bounced back up and began pummeling the challenger, even though, as he later admitted, he had to fight "the rest of the bout in a fog."[35]

A flurry of punches sent Firpo to the canvas. Dempsey, as was his habit, hovered over his foe and immediately continued the attack when Firpo got back to his feet at the count of two. The two fighters continued to slug it out, with Dempsey scoring time and time again. He knocked Firpo down an incredible seven times, but the challenger refused to stay on the mat.

Suddenly, Firpo unleashed a tremendous right to the head that sent Dempsey falling backward through the ropes and out of the ring. With the illegal help of some members of the press corps who were sitting at ringside, the champion climbed back into the ring and managed to hang on until the bell sounded to end the round.

The second round started with Firpo advancing toward Dempsey. The Manassa Mauler managed to avoid Firpo's frantic

minutes. Those four minutes, however, were some of the most action packed in the history of boxing.

Known as the Wild Bull of the Pampas, the former Buenos Aires drugstore clerk swings, and then caught the challenger with a left to the chin to send him down for the eighth time. Incredibly, the Argentinean arose at the count of three. This time, however, he had little left to offer. Another combination by Dempsey sent him to the canvas for the ninth and final time. Firpo was counted out at the fifty-seven-second mark of round two in a bout marked by eleven knockdowns, or an average of one every twenty-two seconds.

Following the fight, Firpo complained loudly that Dempsey had not followed the prefight agreement that a boxer would retreat to a neutral corner in the event of a knockdown. A rule requiring all fighters to do so would eventually go into effect. The decree would have a significant effect on the bout between Dempsey and Gene Tunney in 1927.

1927 Gene Tunney –Jack Dempsey

The September 22, 1927, heavyweight title fight between champion Gene Tunney and former champ Jack Dempsey at Soldier Field in Chicago is perhaps the most famous bout in the history of boxing. In their

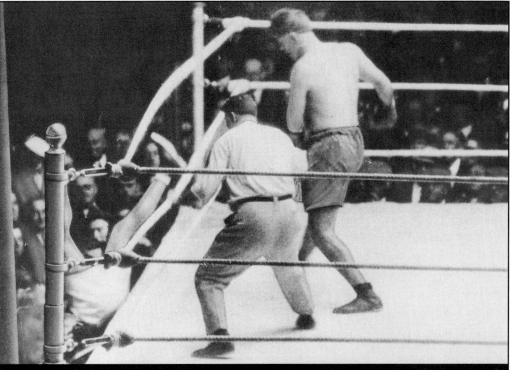

Luis Firpo knocks Jack Dempsey out of the ring in the first round. Dempsey returned to the ring and knocked out Firpo in the second round.

The referee moves Jack Dempsey to the other side of the ring after Dempsey knocked down Gene Tunney. This allowed Tunney enough time to get up and continue the fight.

first meeting the year before, Tunney, the challenger, outboxed the Manassa Mauler to win the crown. The rematch attracted much attention and produced a record gate of $2.65 million.

Prior to the match the fighters were instructed to go to the farthest neutral corner in the event of a knockdown. This was in response to complaints by Tunney's handlers of Dempsey's habit of standing directly over his fallen victims. As the rule mandated:

When a knockdown occurs, the timekeeper shall immediately arise and announce the seconds audibly as they elapse. The referee shall see first that the opponent retires to the farthest neutral corner and then, turning to the timekeeper, shall pick up the count in unison with him, announcing the seconds to the boxer on the floor. Should the boxer on his feet fail to go, or stay, in the corner, the referee and timekeeper shall cease counting until he has so retired.[36]

The fight began, and after six rounds, Tunney was ahead by a comfortable margin. In the first minute of round seven, a flurry of blows sent Tunney to the canvas. Referee Dave Barry began the count before noticing that Dempsey was at his shoulder. He stopped and waved the fighter away. When Dempsey did not move (whether from stubbornness or confusion is a matter of debate), Barry took him by the arm and moved him away. He waited until Dempsey was in the farthest neutral corner—at least five seconds after Tunney had been knocked down—before restarting the count. By the time the fight resumed, Tunney had had at least fourteen seconds to regain his composure. He held off Dempsey's attack and managed to outpoint him over the last three rounds to retain his title.

Whether or not the extra five seconds were vital to Tunney's ability to withstand Dempsey's onslaught is a matter of conjecture. Although the champion said he was not hurt and did not need the extra time, other observers disagreed. George Lytton, one of the two judges, said, "There have been many remarks to the effect that Tunney could have risen sooner. I don't think so. In my opinion Tunney would have been counted out if the ex-champion had moved away faster."[37] More than three-quarters of a century later, the debate still goes on.

1938 Joe Louis
–Max Schmeling

Despite lasting a mere 124 seconds, the 1938 rematch between heavyweight champion Joe Louis and former champ Max Schmeling of Germany is remembered as one of the major sports events of the twentieth century. With World War II looming on the horizon for the United States, the fight was seen by many as a showdown between the forces of good (Louis, representing democracy in the United States) and evil (Schmeling, representing Nazism in Germany).

In their first fight two years before, Schmeling had handed his inexperienced foe the first loss of his professional career. Louis learned from his mistakes and

CHAMPIONSHIP RULES

Although there may be some variation from fight to fight, the basic rules governing championship encounters in the ring are similar for the four major boxing organizations—the World Boxing Association (WBA), World Boxing Council (WBC), World Boxing Organization (WBO), and International Boxing Federation (IBF). The rules for unified championship bouts are as follows:

1. No standing 8 count.
2. No 3 knockdown rule.
3. Fighter cannot be saved by the bell in any round.
4. 10 point must system is in effect.
5. Only the referee can stop the fight.
6. Fight stopped due to accidental head butt:
   a. Technical draw up to and including the fourth round.
   b. Goes to the scorecard after the fourth round.

eventually won the title from James Braddock in June 1937. Now he looked to avenge his only loss while at the same time disproving German dictator Adolf Hitler's ravings of Aryan supremacy. As he wrote in his 1976 biography, "I knew I had to get Schmeling good. I had my own personal reasons and the whole damned country was depending on me."[38]

Louis did not let them down. He exploded from his corner at the opening bell, swarming over the German with a barrage of punches. Louis did not give the challenger a chance to throw his powerful right and sent him to the canvas after only thirty seconds had elapsed. Schmeling got up, but Louis put him down a second time and then a third, administering a vicious beating. Referee Arthur Donovan finally stopped the bout with nearly a minute still remaining in round one. Schmeling had been so dominated that he was only able to throw two punches. As Harry Carpenter writes: "This could well have been the most concentratedly savage punishment meted out by one man to another with fists in the 200-odd years since James Figg began it all. Louis had the look of the finest fighting machine yet produced."[39]

Louis held onto the heavyweight crown for another eleven years, becoming the first African American to emerge as a hero to both blacks and whites alike. Schmeling (who was not in fact a Nazi) was never again a serious contender. Both men served in the military during the war and became friends in later years.

1946 Tony Zale –Rocky Graziano

When legendary ring announcer Don Dunphy was asked to identify the greatest fight of the two thousand or so that he had broadcast, he did not hesitate. He picked the first of the series of three fights between middleweights Tony Zale and Rocky Graziano. The battle between the Man of Steel (Zale had worked in a steel mill before becoming a fighter) and the Dead End Kid (Graziano had grown up on New York City's tough East Side) took place before nearly forty thousand fans in Yankee Stadium on September 27, 1946.

The champion Zale had not fought in four years, having served in the U.S. Navy during World War II. Because of this, Graziano (who was nine years younger) entered the match as an 11-5 favorite. The fighters charged from their corners for round one and Zale drew first blood by connecting with a left hook that sent Graziano to the canvas within the first minute. Graziano bounced right up, however, and fought off Zale's savage attack. Just before the bell ended the round, he staggered the champion with a right to the chin.

Graziano continued his onslaught in round two. He finally decked the champion with a series of right hands, but Zale was

Tony Zale (left) fights Rocky Graziano in Yankee Stadium in 1946. Zale won the match and retained his title.

again saved by the bell. (After the bout, it was discovered that Zale's right thumb had been broken in the round.) Over the next three rounds, Graziano and Zale traded punches, with the challenger's blows doing far more damage. The fifth round ended with Zale looking like a beaten man.

Breathing with difficulty through a bloodied nose, Zale somehow staggered out for round six. As the challenger pressed in for the kill, the champion unleashed one final, powerful right into Graziano's solar plexus. For a moment, he stood there paralyzed until a Zale left hook sent him crashing to the canvas. Wrote Graziano in his autobiography, "That jolt shot from my head to my feet. The feeling went out of my feet and I went whang on the canvas like I didn't have any feet at all."[40] Referee Ruby Goldstein's count reached ten just before Graziano rose to his feet. Looking more like the victor than the vanquished, Graziano tried to return to the fray, but it was too late. Zale had retained the title.

The Zale-Graziano rivalry continued the next July with a rematch before an indoor record crowd of 18,547 at Chicago Stadium. This time, Graziano came back from the brink of defeat to take the championship by stopping Zale in six rounds. The two men fought one more time in June 1948, with Zale becoming the second man in history—Stanley Ketchel being the first—to regain the middleweight title.

1975 Muhammad Ali –Joe Frazier

There was no love lost between Muhammad Ali and Joe Frazier. Ali dismissed Frazier as little more than an animal with taunts such as "gorilla," "ugly," and "ignorant." Frazier viewed Ali as a clown, a fast-talking, dancing, poetry-reciting windbag who was not worthy of the title of world heavyweight champion.

In their first fight in 1971, the champion Frazier defeated Ali, who was making a comeback from his suspension for refusing to enter the army. In their next meeting, when neither one was champ, Ali won on points. This time, Ali held the title and Frazier was the challenger.

The fight before twenty-eight thousand fans in the Philippine Coliseum in Manila began with Ali taking the lead in the early rounds, seemingly hitting Frazier at will. From the fifth round through the tenth, however, Frazier came back and administered a terrific beating to the taller Ali. He staggered Ali with two left hooks to the face in round six, but the former champ withstood the assault. After ten rounds, the fight appeared to be even.

Ali bounced back in round eleven and drew blood from Frazier's mouth. He

THE DEAN OF BOXING REFEREES

A prizefight cannot take place without a referee, and Arthur Mercante Sr. is recognized worldwide as the dean of boxing referees. A former New York Golden Gloves boxer, he began his career refereeing service bouts in the U.S. Navy in 1942. Following his discharge, he continued officiating amateur fights. Ten years later, he moved up to the professional ranks.

Mercante refereed an incredible 137 world title fights in his career, a fact which is even more impressive considering that there were only eight weight classes and one champion per division for much of that time. Included among the fights he officiated were the Floyd Patterson–Ingemar Jo-

hannson match in which Patterson became the first man to regain the heavyweight title, the Fight of the Century between Muhammad Ali and Joe Frazier, and George Foreman's first title bout against Joe Frazier.

Beginning in 2000 Mercante ran specialized training sessions for boxing judges and referees in New York. As State Athletic Commission Chairman Mel Southard said, "For more than half a century, fans of boxing have trusted Arthur Mercante's judgment and those in the boxing industry have been inspired by his high standards." Mercante was inducted into the International Boxing Hall of Fame in 1995.

continued his attack through the twelfth and thirteenth rounds, bombarding Frazier's face with one blow after another but was unable to put him on the canvas. By the fourteenth round, both fighters were clearly exhausted. Ali somehow managed to maintain his assault, but Frazier was unable to defend himself. When he headed back to his corner at the bell, his eyes were practically closed shut from the repeated blows. There was one round remaining, but Frazier's manager, Eddie Futch, would not let him go out.

Too tired to celebrate his victory, Ali dropped to the canvas to rest.

Frazier's valiant effort finally earned him Ali's respect. "I always bring out the best in the men I fight," said the victor, "but Joe Frazier, I'll tell the world right now, brings out the best in me. I'm gonna tell ya, that's one helluva man, and God bless him."[41]

Frazier, too, had words of praise for his opponent. "Man, I hit him with punches that'd bring down the walls of a city," said the defeated warrior. "Lawdy, lawdy, he's a great champion."[42]

CHAPTER 6

Down for the Count?

Although people have called for a ban on boxing for years, it is highly unlikely that what *Sports Illustrated* writer Richard Hoffer called "the cockroach of sport"[43] will ever be made illegal in the United States. That does not mean, however, that the sport is on solid footing.

Sports journalist Pierce Egan once wrote,

It has been the expressed opinion of the fancy that the ancient spirit of nobleness of pugilism, which were wont to prevail, have much degenerated; and the combatants do not appear to possess that fine stamina which so conspicuously marked the days of the above-mentioned pugilists. . . . Pugilism, generally is . . . *in a degenerate state!*[44]

Egan wrote those words in 1912, but his conclusion is shared by many observers today. The sweet science is at its lowest point in years. It faces a multitude of problems that must be addressed if it hopes to be able to approach the level of popularity it once held with sports fans.

Health and Safety Measures

No one denies that boxing is brutal. In no other sport is the objective to physically hurt your opponent as much as possible. One medical study after another has corroborated the damage that is done to the human brain by repeated punches to the head. Although boxing's death rate of 0.13 per 1,000 participants is similar to that of the sports of motorcycle racing, parachuting, and hang gliding, the incidence of nonfatal injuries is much higher. A 1993 report on brain damage in boxers in the *American Journal of Sports Medicine* reported that "dementia pugilistica" (commonly referred to as "punch drunk") affects from 9 to 25 percent of all pro boxers. Symptoms of the condition range from inattention to memory loss to impaired hearing to "a decrease in general cognitive functions."[45] To improve health and safety in boxing, several measures have been suggested.

Protective Gear

Since blows to the head are the cause of the majority of boxing injuries, it would seem to make sense to make headguards mandatory, as they are in all amateur bouts. Some argue, however, that their use would bring about the exact opposite result. They suggest that the bulky gear would give an opponent a larger target and would impair a fighter's vision. Since it absorbs sweat, it would also make a boxer's head heavier, making it more difficult for him to avoid punches. Some even argue that headgear might actually cause greater resonance and movement of

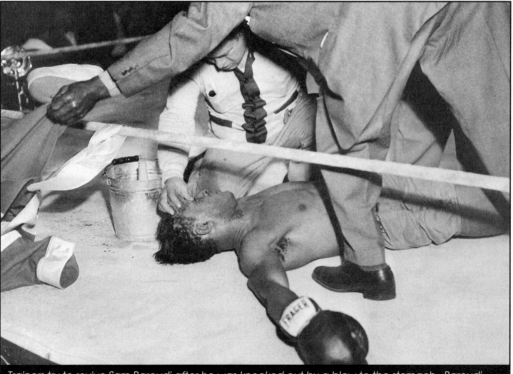

Trainers try to revive Sam Baroudi after he was knocked out by a blow to the stomach. Baroudi later died of a cerebral hemorrhage.

the brain when a blow is landed. In addition, wearing headgear might encourage a false sense of security. Rather than trying to avoid a punch, a boxer might allow himself to be hit, falsely believing the headgear will absorb the full force of the blow.

Another proposal suggests that larger gloves would reduce injuries since more padding would cushion a punch and thereby lessen its force. This, in turn, would result in fewer knockouts. Fewer knockouts, however, most likely would result in longer fights, with boxers receiving more sustained punishment to their bodies. This might lead to a greater likelihood of long-term damage and more severe injuries later in fights.

Other Changes

In addition to changes in the equipment used, other suggestions have also been made to attempt to reduce boxing injuries. One of these is to reduce the number of rounds in a bout. Although this might eliminate the type of serious blood clots that occur in later rounds, it might also encourage fighters to throw more punches and pace themselves less than in a longer fight. This would likely lead to other injuries.

A similar suggestion would be to shorten the length of a round or to increase the time between rounds. Doing so would slow the tempo of the fight. It would also give the participants more time to recover and allow for better medical assessment of injuries. On the other hand, shorter rounds might encourage fighters to take more risks. Although the extra time between rounds would give a boxer a longer time to recover, this might cause him to be subjected to more punishment than if the bout had been stopped.

Making the Weight

Making changes in events that occur prior to a bout might have as much—if not more—impact on a fighter's health and well-being as making changes in the fight itself. Many medical experts believe that one of the key factors involved in serious head injuries is the rapid weight loss some fighters undergo to reach the required maximum weight for a bout. They count on not eating and dehydrating in the days before the weigh-in, believing they can quickly rehydrate in the twenty-four hours before the match, thereby gaining an advantage with extra weight. This could be avoided if weigh-ins were held on the same day as the fight itself. Although this would prevent fighters from being over the weight limit, it would not stop the rapid weight losses before the weigh-in that might lead to a fighter being in a weakened condition for a match and therefore more susceptible to injury.

Despite the calls for improving the safety of the sport, some insist boxing is fine the way it is. Says Simon Block, general secretary of the British Boxing Board of Control, "It is a pure sport and a tough sport but as well as the dangers there are positive sides

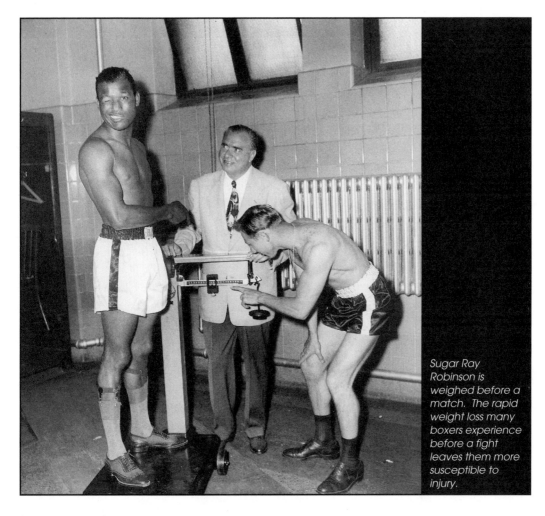

Sugar Ray Robinson is weighed before a match. The rapid weight loss many boxers experience before a fight leaves them more susceptible to injury.

such as developing discipline and character and it gives the chance for a fighter to prove himself man to man. That overrides the dangers of the sport."[46]

A National Commission

Although many may align themselves with Block on the issue of safety, no one denies that boxing is still in need of improvement in many other areas. Boxing is like no other major professional sport. It is completely unregulated, with no federal body to enforce rules and regulations in the areas of health, safety, and economics. State commissions (where they exist) are often filled with unqualified people. They are loosely organized under the Association of Boxing Commissions (ABC), but there is still a lack of uniformity and consistency from one state to another.

A glaring example of that lack of uniformity occurred in 2002 when Mike Tyson attempted to obtain a license for a bout with heavyweight champion Lennox Lewis. As described by Patrick B. Fife in the *Hofstra Law Review*, "The ABC had requested that none of its members grant Tyson a license due to his violent and criminal activity outside the ring and his violent and unsportsmanlike conduct inside the ring. Nevada, Texas, Colorado, West Virginia, and Georgia all followed the ABC and refused to license Tyson. However, fellow ABC members [of] Tennessee, the eventual site of the bout, and Washington, D.C., agreed to license Tyson."[47]

Many observers feel only a federal organization can ensure that the interests of fans and boxers alike are being protected. It has been proven time and again that those currently in control have been unable—or unwilling—to do so.

Corruption

In decades past, corruption in boxing generally took the form of fixed fights. The outcome of matches was prearranged in order to enable gamblers to make betting coups. "The corruption now," wrote veteran political reporter Jack Newfield in 2001, "is more subtle, sophisticated and systemic. It depends more on fixing the rankings than fixing the fights, although some rigging of results does go on, to manufacture 'white hopes.'"[48]

Rankings are issued by the major sanctioning bodies in boxing today, including the World Boxing Association, the World Boxing Council, and the International Boxing Federation. Fighters

NEW YORK'S RING 8

Professional boxing is the only major sport that does not have a union to provide benefits for its retired members. An attempt was made to form such an organization in 1953 when the Veteran Boxers' Association (VBA) came into existence. Chapters were eventually formed in various cities, including Ring 8 in New York. (New York was the eighth city on the list.)

As stated in the organization's charter, the purpose of the VBA was to "foster, promote and perpetuate a spirit of benevolent fraternity and charity among active and inactive valid professional boxers, and to provide for the physical, mental and monetary welfare of indigent professional boxers." Although most of the VBA's "Rings" have long since been dissolved, New York's Ring 8 continues to function. It has helped hundreds of former fighters, providing them with—among other things—medical examinations and a $500 death benefit. It also awards the Bill Gallo College Scholarship to a qualified boxer who desires to further his education. The organization's membership in recent years has been supplemented by boxing fans and supporters who have joined as associate members.

are ranked from one to ten—presumably according to ability—with a top ranking virtually guaranteeing a lucrative championship bout. Unfortunately such rankings are subjective by nature and open to corruption. Newfield describes a 1997 FBI investigation that uncovered bribes paid to former IBF president Robert Lee. Doug Beavers, IBF ratings committee chairman responsible for issuing the ratings, became an informant for Assistant U.S. Attorney Jose Sierra. He helped prosecutors gather some two hundred hours of undercover video and audio tapes. Despite overwhelming evidence of bribery (well-known promoter Bob Arums admitted paying $100,000 to the IBF in order to get the group's sanction of a fight), a jury convicted Lee of nothing more than money laundering and tax fraud.

The ranking organizations are also taken to task for their ignorance in preparing rankings. A blatant example of this occurred in the case of super middleweight Darwin Morris. Morris last fought in July 1999. Nine months later, he appeared at No. 10 in the ratings of the World Boxing Organization (WBO). After dropping to No. 11 in July 2000, he advanced to No. 9 in August, No. 7 in October, and then jumped two more times before peaking at No. 5 in the January 2001 rankings. His high standing came as something of a shock to those who knew Morris. Unlike the WBO, they were aware that he had died of HIV-related meningitis in October 2000. Said WBO president Francisco Valcarcel after being told the news, "It is sometimes hard to get all the information on boxers, and we obviously missed the fact that Darwin was dead. It is regrettable."[49]

Fixed Fights

Corruption dealing with fixed fights stems from the fact that the great majority of dominant fighters in recent years have been either African American or Hispanic. (This is also partly responsible for the decreasing interest in the sport among a large percentage of the population. As Arums admitted, "Only among Hispanics is boxing still a major sport."[50]) As a result, fights nowadays are occasionally fixed in order to build up the reputation of some white heavyweights promoted as "white hopes." The fixing might not be as obvious as predetermining the outcome of a match. By manipulating who a fighter meets in the ring, however, the results are basically the same. Promoters can do this by matching someone against an opponent who is obviously unqualified. In this way, a fighter's record can be padded to make him appear much better than he really is. Promoter Don King has been accused of having done this with boxers such as Chuck Wepner, Gerry Cooney,

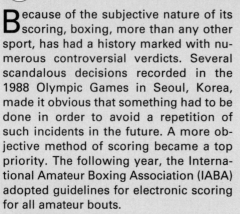

COMPUTERIZED SCORING

Because of the subjective nature of its scoring, boxing, more than any other sport, has had a history marked with numerous controversial verdicts. Several scandalous decisions recorded in the 1988 Olympic Games in Seoul, Korea, made it obvious that something had to be done in order to avoid a repetition of such incidents in the future. A more objective method of scoring became a top priority. The following year, the International Amateur Boxing Association (IABA) adopted guidelines for electronic scoring for all amateur bouts.

Under the traditional scoring system, the judges assess the value of each blow and mentally award points to the fighters. The winner of a round is given twenty points, with somewhat less going to the loser. At the end of the match, the scores are added to determine the winner.

With computerized scoring, the outcome is determined in a more objective manner. Each judge works a keypad that features four buttons—red and blue for scoring, and red and blue warning buttons. When a judge sees a clean scoring punch, he presses the button for the fighter who landed it. Three of the five judges must press the same colored button within a one-second interval in order for the blow to be recorded as part of the official score. (The interval begins when the first judge records the punch.) If a fighter receives a warning for a foul, the referee notifies the judges. If a judge agrees, he pushes the warning button for that boxer. If a majority of the judges agree with the referee, two points are added to the opponent's score. The winner of the bout is the fighter who tallies the most scoring punches.

Although electronic scoring is not perfect, it has received a favorable response. Boxers have greater confidence that they will receive a fair decision, and the number of protests and complaints has dropped drastically.

and Peter McNeeley. Although not illegal, such maneuvering may prevent other more deserving fighters from achieving their dreams.

Conflicts of Interest

Conflicts of interest between promoters and managers offer other potential opportunities for corruption. As Newfield explains,

> In theory, a manager is supposed to negotiate the most favorable economic terms for his fighter, while the promoter

is supposed to make the largest possible profit on the event. But there have been dozens of fights in which Carl King managed both fighters while the match was promoted by his father, Don King, boxing's dominant promoter since 1974, accumulating a net worth of $200 million along the way. Bob Arum has also had similar conflicts of interest.

> If the promoter's son represents both fighters, what chance does the boxer have of getting paid fairly?[51]

Julio Cesar Chavez (left) and Don King (right) celebrate Chavez's victory over Refugio Rojas in 1986.

As Lou Diablo—former senior vice president for Home Box Office (HBO) Boxing—told Newfield, "The current system is designed for abuse. It is set up to keep the fighter in the dark. No one is looking out for the fighter's economic interest."[52] This, too, would hopefully be remedied by the formation of a national commission.

A Shrinking Talent Pool

Even a national commission, however, would not be able to reverse the effects of the shrinking pool of boxing talent. With Mike Tyson on the downside of his career, there are few marquee names in the heavyweight division to turn the sport's image around. As Bert Sugar, former editor of *The Ring* and *Boxing Illustrated*, once explained, "Bottom line—as the heavyweight division goes, so goes boxing. This goes back to John Sullivan. And it has something to do with being American. Americans are always obsessed with big things."[53] With fewer prominent names in the heavyweight division, fewer people follow the sport, and boxing's image remains tarnished.

Not as many big men go into boxing nowadays since there is surer, safer money to be made in other sports. Fewer youngsters see any attraction in spending hours in a gym getting hit in the head. The result is that there are fewer boxing clubs in existence than there used to be, making it harder for those who are interested to find venues where they can perfect their craft. It is harder still to find good trainers to help develop young fighters. Explained Emanuel Steward, founder of Detroit's famous Crank Boxing Team, "Not many ex-fighters are taking up the training profession anymore. They don't want to go through the apprenticeship. I see guys get frustrated when they're teaching because they want to box again themselves. They start saying, 'Wait, *I* can beat this kid.' Other times, you discover that a guy who won strictly on natural talent when he was competing just isn't capable of teaching fundamentals. Defense, especially, is a lost art."[54]

Despite these problems, there is still much excitement to be found in the lower weight classes where most of the better fighters are Hispanic. Boxing still has an attraction for youngsters from poorer neighborhoods who see it as one of their few hopes of escaping the ghetto. The result, according to Diablo, is that "The sport is dying among English-speaking Americans."[55]

A Shrinking Audience

Ironically, while boxing still offers hope of a better life for underprivileged youngsters, it has become more and more inaccessible to the average fan. Where boxing on network television was common in the 1950s and 1960s, it has become increasingly rare. Explained former ABC analyst (now ABC president) Alex Wallau, "The networks make

BOXING DEATHS

Although the American Medical Association Council on Medical Affairs has said that deaths due to boxing occur at the rate of just 0.13 per 1,000 fighters, the rate usually seems higher. This is perhaps due to the high-profile fatalities that occur, occasionally even to champions. Among the more notable boxers to die in the ring are the following:

Luther McCarty, May 24, 1913—Generally recognized as the white heavyweight champion of the world, McCarty was killed by a blow delivered less than two minutes into the first round of his bout with Arthur Pelkey. Favored in the match, McCarty died as a result of a blow to the chest, although it is possible a previous injury suffered in a fall from a horse may have been responsible.

Jimmy Doyle, June 25, 1947—Doyle was killed in a welterweight championship bout with Sugar Ray Robinson. Blows to the jaw and face by the champion caused a cerebral hemorrhage that took Doyle's life the day after his eighth-round knockout.

Benny "Kid" Paret, April 3, 1962—Welterweight champion Paret died nine days after losing his title to Emile Griffith. The champion collapsed in the twelfth round of the nationally televised match and never regained consciousness.

Davey Moore, March 25, 1963—Moore became the second champion to die in the ring within a year when he passed

Davey Moore died in the ring when a ring rope struck the back of his skull.

away the morning after his title match with Sugar Ramos. The fatal injury was not caused by a punch but rather by a blow to the back of the skull, by a snapping ring rope Moore fell against in the last thirty seconds of the fight. The coroner, however, reported that blows to the jaw could not be ruled out as a contributing factor in the death.

long-term deals with the NFL [National Football League] and the figure-skating organizations, but boxing is the only sport negotiated on an event-by-event basis. It's always easier to push it aside because there's not a long-term commitment to it."[56] The bouts that do appear are generally between second-rate fighters. The networks simply cannot compete for the better matchups with cable outputs like HBO, Showtime, and pay-per-view.

Seeing a high-profile bout in person is even less likely. The top battles are held in the casino hotels of Las Vegas or Atlantic City that can guarantee promoters millions of dollars by paying a site fee to host the event. In addition to the cost of traveling to the site, a fan might have to lay out hundreds of dollars for even the cheapest seats at these high-profile venues.

Prospects for the Future

Boxing has clearly seen better times. The problems it has faced over the years may have changed, but they have not lessened. The sport endured in the past even when it was illegal. Many of the problems it faces now, however, are monetary in nature. Greed and avarice have always been difficult to overcome. Unfortunately boxing faces a long, hard, uphill battle if it is to regain the degree of popularity it held in the past.

Awards and Statistics

Organization Abbreviations

IBF- International Boxing Federation **USBF**- United States Boxing Federation **WBC**- World Boxing Council
NBA- National Boxing Association **WBA**- World Boxing Association **WBO**- World Boxing Organization

Champion	Organization	Year
Strawweight Champions (105 pounds)		
Jum-Hwan Choi	(IBF)	1986–88
Tacy Macalos	(IBF)	1988–89
German Torres	(WBC)	1988–89
Yul-Woo Lee	(WBC)	1989
Muangchai Kittikasem	(IBF)	1989–90
Humberto Gonzalez	(WBC)	1989–90
Michael Carbajal	(IBF)	1990
Rolando Pascua	(WBC)	1990
Melchor Cob Castro	(WBC)	1991
Ricardo Lopez	(WBC)	1990–98
Ratanapol Voraphin	(IBF)	1992–97
Chana Porpaoin	(WBA)	1993–95
Rosendo Alvarez	(WBA)	1995–98
Ricardo Lopez	(WBA, WBC)	1998–99
Zolani Petelo	(IBF)	1997–2001
Wandee Chor Chareon	(WBC)	1999–2000
Noel Arambulet	(WBA)	1999–2000
Joma Gamboa	(WBA)	2000
Keitaro Hoshino	(WBA)	2000–01
Jose Antonio Aguirre	(WBC)	2000
Chana Porpaoin	(WBA)	2001
Robert Leyva	(IBF)	2001–02
Yutaka Niida	(WBA)	2001
Keitaro Hoshino	(WBA)	2002
Noel Arambulent	(WBA)	2002–
Miguel Barrera	(IBF)	2002–

Junior Flyweight Champions (108 pounds)

Champion	Organization	Year
Franco Udella	(WBC)	1975
Jaime Rios	(WBA)	1975–76

Champion	Organization	Year
Luis Estaba	(WBC)	1975–78
Juan Guzman	(WBA)	1976
Yoko Gushiken	(WBA)	1976–81
Freddy Castillo	(WBC)	1978
Netrnoi Vorasingh	(WBC)	1978
Sung-Jun Kim	(WBC)	1978–80
Shigeo Nakajima	(WBC)	1980
Hilario Zapata	(WBC)	1980–82
Pedro Flores	(WBA)	1981
Hwan-Jin Kim	(WBA)	1981
Katsuo Tokashiki	(WBA)	1981–83
Amado Urzua	(WBC)	1982
Tadashi Tomori	(WBC)	1982
Hilario Zapata	(WBC)	1982–83
Jung-Koo Chang	(WBC)	1983–88
Lupe Madera	(WBA)	1983–84
Dodie Penalosa	(IBF)	1983–86
Francisco Quiroz	(WBA)	1984–85
Joey Olivo	(WBA)	1985
Myung-Woo Yuh	(WBA)	1985–91
Jum-Hwan Choi	(IBF)	1986–88
Tacy Macalos	(IBF)	1988–89
German Torres	(WBC)	1988–89
Yul-Woo Lee	(WBC)	1989
Muangchai Kittikasem	(IBF)	1989–90
Humberto Gonzalez	(WBC)	1989–90
Michael Carbajal	(IBF)	1990–94
Rolando Pascua	(WBC)	1990
Melchor Cob Castro	(WBC)	1991
Humberto Gonzalez	(WBC)	1991–93
Hirokia Ioka	(WBA)	1991–92
Michael Carbajal	(WBC)	1993–94
Myung-Woo Yuh	(WBA)	1993
Leo Gamez	(WBA)	1993–95

Champion	Organization	Year
Humberto Gonzalez	(WBC, IBF)	1994–95
Choi Hi-Yong	(WBA)	1995–96
Saman Sor Jaturong	(WBC, IBF)	1995–96
Carlos Murillo	(WBA)	1996
Keiji Yamaguchi	(WBA)	1996
Michael Carbajal	(IBF)	1996–97
Saman Sor Jaturong	(WBC)	1995–99
Phichit Chor Siriwat	(WBA)	1996–2000
Mauricio Pastrana	(IBF)	1997–98
Will Grigsby	(IBF)	1999
Choi Yo-Sam	(WBC)	1999–2002
Ricardo Lopez	(IBF)	1999–2000
Beibis Mendoza	(WBA)	2000–01
Rosendo Alvarez	(WBA)	2001–
Jorge Arce	(WBC)	2002–

Flyweight Champions (112 pounds)

Champion	Organization	Year
Sid Smith		1913
Bill Ladbury		1913–14
Percy Jones		1914
Joe Symonds		1914–16
Jimmy Wilde		1916–23
Pancho Villa		1923–25
Fidel Labarba		1925–27
Frenchy Belanger	(NBA)	1927–28
Izzy Schwartz		1927–29
Johnny McCoy		1927–28
Newsboy Brown		1928
Frankie Genaro	(NBA)	1928–29
Johnny Hill		1928–29
Spider Pladner	(NBA)	1929
Frankie Genaro	(NBA)	1929–31
Willie Lamorte		1929–30
Midget Wolgast		1930–35
Young Perez	(NBA)	1931–32
Jackie Brown	(NBA)	1932–35
Benny Lynch		1935–38
Small Montana		1935–37
Peter Kane		1938–43
Little Dado	(NBA)	1938–40
Jackie Paterson		1943–48
Rinty Monaghan		1948–50
Terry Allen		1950
Salvador (Dado) Marino		1950–52
Yoshio Shirai		1953–54
Pascual Perez		1954–60

Champion	Organization	Year
Pone Kingpetch		1960–62
Masahiko (Fighting) Harada		1962–63
Pone Kingpetch		1963
Hiroyuki Ebihara		1963–64
Pone Kingpetch		1964–65
Salvatore Burrini		1965–66
Horacio Accavallo	(WBA)	1966–68
Walter McGowan		1966
Chartchai Chionoi		1966–69
Efren Torres		1969–70
Hiroyuki Ebihara	(WBA)	1969
Bernabe Villacampo	(WBA)	1969–70
Chartchai Chionoi		1970
Berkrerk Chartvanchai	(WBA)	1970
Masao Ohba	(WBA)	1970–73
Erbito Salavarria		1970–73
Betulio Gonzalez	(WBC)	1972
Venice Borkorsor	(WBC)	1972–73
Venice Borkorsor		1973
Chartchai Chionoi	(WBA)	1973–74
Betulio Gonzalez	(WBA)	1973–74
Shoji Oguma	(WBC)	1974–75
Susumu Hanagata	(WBA)	1974–75
Miguel Canto	(WBC)	1975–79
Erbito Salavarria	(WBA)	1975–76
Alfonso Lopez	(WBA)	1976
Guty Espadas	(WBA)	1976–78
Betulio Gonzalez	(WBA)	1978–79
Chan-Hee Park	(WBC)	1979–80
Luis Ibarra	(WBA)	1979–80
Tae-Shik Kim	(WBA)	1980
Shoji Oguma	(WBC)	1980–81
Peter Mathebula	(WBA)	1980–81
Santos Laciar	(WBA)	1981
Antonio Avelar	(WBC)	1981–82
Luis Ibarra	(WBA)	1981
Juan Herrera	(WBA)	1981–82
Prudencio Cardona	(WBC)	1982
Santos Laciar	(WBA)	1982–85
Freddie Castillo	(WBC)	1982
Eleoncio Mercedes	(WBC)	1982–83
Charlie Magri	(WBC)	1983
Frank Cedeno	(WBC)	1983–84
Soon-Chun Kwon	(IBF)	1983–85
Koji Kobayashi	(WBC)	1984
Gabriel Bernal	(WBC)	1984
Sot Chitalada	(WBC)	1984–88

Champion	Organization	Year	Champion	Organization	Year
Hilario Zapate	(WBA)	1985–87	Payao Poontarat	(WBC)	1983–84
Chong-Kwan Chung	(IBF)	1985–86	Joo-Do Chun	(IBF)	1983–85
Bi-Won Chung	(IBF)	1986	Jiro Watanabe		1984–86
Hi-Sup Shin	(IBF)	1986–87	Kaosai Galaxy	(WBA)	1984
Dodie Penalosa	(IBF)	1987	Ellyas Pical	(IBF)	1985–86
Fidel Bassa	(WBA)	1987–89	Cesar Polanco	(IBF)	1986
Choi Chang-Ho	(IBF)	1987–88	Gilberto Roman		1986–87
Rolando Bohol	(IBF)	1988	Ellyas Pical	(IBF)	1986
Yong-Kang Kim	(WBC)	1988–89	Santos Laciar	(WBC)	1987
Duke McKenzie	(IBF)	1988–89	Tae-Il Chang	(IBF)	1987
Dave McAuley	(IBF)	1989–92	Sugar Rojas	(WBC)	1987–88
Sot Chitalada	(WBC)	1989–91	Ellyas Pical	(IBF)	1987–89
Jesus Rojas	(WBA)	1989–90	Gilberto Roman	(WBC)	1988–89
Yul-Woo Lee	(WBA)	1990	Juan Polo Perez	(IBF)	1989–90
Leopard Tamakuma	(WBA)	1990–91	Nana Konadu	(WBC)	1989–90
Muangchai Kittikasem	(WBC)	1991–92	Sung-Kil Moon	(WBC)	1990–93
Yong-Kang Kim	(WBA)	1991–92	Robert Quiroga	(IBF)	1990–93
Rodolfo Blanco	(IBF)	1992	Julio Borboa	(IBF)	1993–94
Yuri Arbachakov	(WBC)	1992–97	Katsuya Onizuka	(WBA)	1993–94
Aquiles Guzman	(WBA)	1992	Lee Hyung-Chul	(WBA)	1994–95
Phichit Sithbangprachan	(IBF)	1992–94	Jose Luis Bueno	(WBC)	1993–94
David Griman	(WBA)	1992–94	Hiroshi Kawashima	(WBC)	1994–97
Saen Sor Ploenchit	(WBA)	1994–96	Harold Grey	(IBF)	1994–95
Francisco Tejedor	(IBF)	1995	Alimi Goitia	(WBA)	1995–96
Danny Romero	(IBF)	1995–96	Yokthai Sith-Oar	(WBA)	1996–97
Mark Johnson	(IBF)	1996–99	Carlos Salazar	(IBF)	1995–96
Jose Bonilla	(WBA)	1996–97	Harold Grey	(IBF)	1996
Chatchai Sasakul	(WBC)	1997–98	Danny Romero	(IBF)	1996–97
Hugo Soto	(WBA)	1998–99	Gerry Penalosa	(WBC)	1997–98
Manny Pacquiao	(WBC)	1998–99	Johnny Tapia	(IBF)	1997–98
Irene Pacheco	(IBF)	1999–	Satoshi Lida	(WBA)	1997–98
Leo Gamez	(WBA)	1999	Cho In-Joo	(WBC)	1998–2000
Medgoen Lukchaopormasak	(WBC)	1999–2000	Jesus Rojas	(WBA)	1998–99
Sornpichai Kratindaenggym	(WBA)	1999–2000	Mark Johnson	(IBF)	1999–2000
Eric Morel	(WBA)	2000–	Hideki Todaka	(WBA)	1999–2000
Malcolm Tunacao	(WBC)	2000–01	Masanori Tokuyama	(WBC)	2000–
Pongsaklek Wonjongkam	(WBC)	2001–	Felix Machado	(IBF)	2000–
			Leo Gamez	(WBA)	2000–01
			Celes Kobayashi	(WBA)	2001–02
			Alexander Munoz	(WBA)	2002–

Junior Bantamweight Champions (115 pounds)

Champion	Organization	Year
Rafael Orono	(WBC)	1980–81
Chul-Ho Kim	(WBC)	1981–82
Gustavo Ballas	(WBA)	1981
Rafael Pedroza	(WBA)	1981–82
Jiro Watanabe	(WBA)	1982–84
Rafael Orono	(WBC)	1982–83

Bantamweight Champions (118 pounds)

Champion	Organization	Year
Tommy (Spider) Kelly		1887
Hughey Boyle		1887–88
Tommy (Spider) Kelly		1889
Chappie Moran		1889–90

Champion	Organization	Year	Champion	Organization	Year
Tommy (Spider) Kelly		1890–92	Manuel Ortiz		1947–50
George Dixon (Claimant)		1890–91	Vic Toweel		1950–52
Billy Plummer		1892–95	Jimmy Carruthers		1952–54
Jimmy Barry		1894–99	Robert Cohen		1954–56
Pedlar Palmer		1895–99	Raul Macias	(NBA)	1955–57
Terry McGovern		1899–1900	Mario D'agata		1956–57
Harry Harris		1901–02	Alphonse Halimi		1957–59
Danny Dougherty		1900–01	Joe Becerra		1959–60
Harry Forbes		1901–03	Johnny Caldwell	(EBU)	1961–62
Frankie Neil		1903–04	Eder Jofre		1961–65
Joe Bowker		1904–05	Masahiko Fighting Harada		1965–68
Jimmy Walsh		1905–06	Lionel Rose		1968–69
Owen Moran (Claimant)		1907–08	Ruben Olivares		1969–70
Monte Attell (Claimant)		1909–10	Chucho Castillo		1970–71
Frankie Conley (Claimant)		1910–11	Ruben Olivares		1971–72
Johnny Coulon		1911–14	Rafael Herrera		1972
Digger Stanley		1910–12	Enrique Pinder		1972–73
Charles Ledoux		1912–13	Romeo Anaya		1973
Eddie Campi		1913–14	Rafael Herrera	(WBC)	1973–74
Kid Williams		1914–17	Arnold Taylor		1973–74
Johnny Ertle (Claimant)		1915–18	Soo-Hwan Hong		1974–75
Pete Herman		1917–20	Rodolfo Martinez	(WBC)	1974–76
Memphis Pal Moore (Claimant)		1918–19	Alfonso Zamora		1975–77
Joe Lynch		1920–21	Carlos Zarate	(WBC)	1976–79
Pete Herman		1921	Jorge Lujan		1977–80
Johnny Buff		1921–22	Lupe Pintor	(WBC)	1979–83
Joe Lynch		1922–24	Julian Solis		1980
Abe Goldstein		1924	Jeff Chandler		1980–84
Cannonball Eddie Martin		1924–25	Albert Davila	(WBC)	1983–85
Phil Rosenberg		1925–27	Richard Sandoval		1984–86
Teddy Baldock		1927	Satoshi Shingaki	(IBF)	1984–85
Bud Taylor	(NBA)	1927–28	Jeff Fenech	(IBF)	1985
Willie Smith		1927–28	Daniel Zaragoza	(WBC)	1985
Bushy Graham		1928–29	Miguel (Happy) Lora	(WBC)	1985–88
Panama Al Brown		1929–35	Gaby Canizales		1986
Sixto Escobar	(NBA)	1934–35	Bernardo Pinango		1986–87
Baltazar Sangchilli		1935–36	Wilfredo Vasquez	(WBA)	1987–88
Lou Salica	(NBA)	1935	Kevin Seabrooks	(IBF)	1987–88
Sixto Escobar	(NBA)	1935–36	Kaokor Galaxy	(WBA)	1988
Tony Marino		1936	Moon Sung-Kil	(WBA)	1988–89
Sixto Escobar		1936–37	Kaokor Galaxy	(WBA)	1989
Harry Jeffra		1937–38	Raul Perez	(WBC)	1988–91
Sixto Escobar		1938–39	Orlando Canizales	(IBF)	1988–94
Georgie Pace	(NBA)	1939–40	Luisito Espinosa	(WBA)	1989–91
Lou Salica		1940–42	Greg Richardson		1991
Manuel Ortiz		1942–47	Joichiro Tatsuyoshi	(WBC)	1991–92
Harold Dade		1947	Israel Contreras	(WBA)	1991–92

Champion	Organization	Year
Eddie Cook	(WBA)	1992
Victor Rabanales	(WBC)	1992–93
Jorge Julio	(WBA)	1992–93
Jung-Il Byun	(WBC)	1993
Junior Jones	(WBA)	1993–94
Yasuei Yakushiji	(WBC)	1993–95
John M. Johnson	(WBA)	1994
Daorung Chuvatana	(WBA)	1994–95
Harold Mestre	(IBF)	1995
Mbuelo Botile	(IBF)	1995–97
Wayne McCullough	(WBC)	1995–96
Veeraphol Sahaprom	(WBA)	1995–96
Nana Yaw Konadu	(WBA)	1996
Daorung Chuvatana	(WBA)	1996–97
Nana Yaw Konadu	(WBA)	1997–98
Sirimongkol Singmanassak	(WBC)	1996–97
Tim Austin	(IBF)	1997–2000
Joichiro Tatsuyoshi	(WBC)	1997–98
Johnny Tapia	(WBA)	1998–99
Veerapol Sahaprom	(WBC)	1998–2000
Paulie Ayala	(WBA)	1999–2001
Eidy Moya	(WBA)	2001–02
Johnny Bredahl	(WBA)	2002–

Junior Featherweight Champions (122 pounds)

Champion	Organization	Year
Jack (Kid) Wolfe		1922–23
Carl Duane		1923–24
Rigoberto Riasco	(WBC)	1976
Royal Kobayashi	(WBC)	1976
Dong-Kyun Yum	(WBC)	1976–77
Wilfredo Gomez	(WBC)	1977–83
Soo-Hwan Hong	(WBA)	1977–78
Ricardo Cardona	(WBA)	1978–80
Leo Randolph	(WBA)	1980
Sergio Palma	(WBA)	1980–82
Leonardo Cruz	(WBA)	1982–84
Jaime Garza	(WBC)	1983
Bobby Berna	(IBF)	1983–84
Loris Stecca	(WBA)	1984
Seung-Il Suh	(IBF)	1984–85
Victor Callejas	(WBA)	1984–85
Juan (Kid) Meza	(WBC)	1984–85
Ji-Woo Kim	(IBF)	1985–86
Lupe Pintor	(WBC)	1985–86
Samart Payakaroon	(WBC)	1986–87

Champion	Organization	Year
Seung-Hoon Lee	(IBF)	1987–88
Louie Espinoza	(WBA)	1987
Jeff French	(WBC)	1987
Julio Gervacio	(WBA)	1987–88
Daniel Zaragoza	(WBC)	1988–90
Jose Sanabria	(IBF)	1988–90
Bernardo Pinango	(WBA)	1988
Juan Jose Estrada	(WBA)	1988–89
Fabrice Benichou	(IBF)	1989–90
Jesus Salud	(WBA)	1989–90
Welcome Ncita	(IBF)	1990–92
Paul Banke	(WBC)	1990
Luis Mendoza	(WBA)	1990–91
Raul Perez	(WBA)	1992
Pedro Decima	(WBC)	1990–91
Kiyoshi Hatanaka	(WBC)	1991
Daniel Zaragoza	(WBC)	1991–92
Tracy Patterson	(WBC)	1992–94
Kennedy McKinney	(IBF)	1993–94
Wilfredo Vasquez	(WBA)	1992–95
Vuyani Bungu	(IBF)	1994–99
Hector Acero Sanchez	(WBC)	1994–95
Antonio Cermeno	(WBA)	1995–98
Daniel Zaragoza	(WBC)	1995–97
Erik Morales	(WBC)	1997–2000
Enrique Sanchez	(WBA)	1998
Nestor Garza	(WBA)	1998–2000
Lehlohonolo Ledwaba	(IBF)	1999–2001
Clarence Adams	(WBA)	2000–01
Willie Jorrin	(WBC)	2000–
Manny Pacquiao	(IBF)	2001–
Yorber Ortega	(WBA)	2001–02
Yoddamrong Sithyodthong	(WBA)	2002
Osamu Sato	(WBA)	2002
Salim Medjkoune	(WBA)	2002–

Featherweight Champions (126 pounds)

Champion	Year
Torpedo Billy Murphy	1890
Young Griffo	1890–92
George Dixon	1892–97
Solly Smith	1897–98
Ben Jordan	1898–99
Eddie Santry	1899–1900
Dave Sullivan	1898
George Dixon	1898–1900
Terry McGovern	1900–01

Champion	Organization	Year	Champion	Organization	Year
Young Corbett II		1901–04	Johnny Famechon	(WBC)	1969–70
Jimmy Britt		1904	Vicente Saldivar	(WBC)	1970
Abe Attell		1904	Kuniaki Shibata	(WBC)	1970–72
Brooklyn Tommy Sullivan		1904–05	Antonio Gomez	(WBA)	1971–72
Abe Attell		1906–12	Clemente Sanchez	(WBC)	1972
Johnny Kilbane		1912–23	Ernesto Marcel	(WBA)	1972–74
Jem Driscoll		1912–13	Jose Legra	(WBC)	1972–73
Eugene Criqui		1923	Eder Jofre	(WBC)	1973–74
Johnny Dundee		1923–24	Ruben Olivares	(WBA)	1974
Louis (Kid) Kaplan		1925–26	Bobby Chacon	(WBC)	1974–75
Dick Finnegan		1926–27	Alexis Arguello	(WBA)	1974–76
Benny Bass		1927–28	Ruben Olivares	(WBC)	1975
Tony Canzoneri		1928	David (Poison) Kotey	(WBC)	1975–76
Andre Routis		1928–29	Danny (Little Red) Lopez	(WBC)	1976–80
Battling Battalino		1929–32	Rafael Ortega	(WBA)	1977
Tommy Paul	(NBA)	1932–33	Cecilio Lastra	(WBA)	1977–78
Kid Chocolate		1932–33	Eusebio Pedroza	(WBA)	1978–85
Freddie Miller	(NBA)	1933–36	Salvador Sanchez	(WBC)	1980–82
Baby Arizmendi		1935–36	Juan Laporte	(WBC)	1982–84
Mike Belloise		1936–37	Wilfredo Gomez	(WBC)	1984
Petey Sarron	(NBA)	1936–37	Min-Keun Oh	(IBF)	1984–85
Henry Armstrong		1937–38	Azumah Nelson	(WBC)	1984–88
Joey Archibald		1938–39	Barry McGuigan	(WBA)	1985–86
Leo Rodak	(NBA)	1938–39	Ki-Young Chung	(IBF)	1985–86
Joey Archibald		1939–40	Steve Cruz	(WBA)	1986–87
Petey Scalzo	(NBA)	1940–41	Antonio Rivera	(IBF)	1986–88
Jimmy Perrin		1940–41	Antonio Esparragoza	(WBA)	1987–91
Harry Jeffra		1940–41	Calvin Grove	(IBF)	1988
Joey Archibald		1941	Jorge Paez	(IBF)	1988–91
Richie Lemos	(NBA)	1941	Jeff Fenech	(WBC)	1988–90
Chalky Wright		1941–42	Marcos Villasana	(WBC)	1990–91
Jackie Wilson	(NBA)	1941–43	Yung-Kyun Park	(WBA)	1991–93
Willie Pep		1942–48	Troy Dorsey	(IBF)	1991
Jackie Callura	(NBA)	1943	Manuel Medina	(IBF)	1991–93
Phil Terranova	(NBA)	1943–44	Paul Hodkinson	(WBC)	1991–93
Sal Bartolo	(NBA)	1944–46	Tom Johnson	(IBF)	1993–97
Sandy Saddler		1948–49	Goyo Vargas	(WBC)	1993
Willie Pep		1949–50	Kevin Kelley	(WBC)	1993–95
Sandy Saddler		1950–57	Eloy Rojas	(WBA)	1993–96
Hogan (Kid) Bassey		1957–59	Alejandro Gonzalez	(WBC)	1995
Davey Moore		1959–63	Manuel Medina	(WBC)	1995–96
Ultiminio (Sugar) Ramos		1963–64	Wilfredo Vasquez	(WBA)	1996–98
Vicente Saldivar		1964–67	Luisito Espinosa	(WBC)	1995–99
Howard Winstone		1968	Naseem Hamed	(IBF)	1997
Raul Rojas	(WBA)	1968	Hector Lizarraga	(IBF)	1997–98
Jose Legra	(WBC)	1968–69	Freddie Norwood	(WBA)	1998
Shozo Saijyo	(WBA)	1968–71	Manuel Medina	(IBF)	1998–99

Champion	Organization	Year
Antonio Cermeno	(WBA)	1998–99
Cesar Soto	(WBC)	1999–2000
Paul Ingle	(IBF)	1999–2000
Mbuelo Botile	(IBF)	2000–01
Guty Espadas	(WBC)	2000–01
Freddie Norwood	(WBA)	1999–2000
Derrick Gainer	(WBA)	2000–
Erik Morales	(WBC)	2001–02
Frankie Toledo	(IBF)	2001
Manuel Medina	(IBF)	2001–02
Johnny Tapia	(IBF)	2002

Junior Lightweight Champions (130 pounds)

Champion	Organization	Year
Johnny Dundee		1921–23
Jack Bernstein		1923
Johnny Dundee		1923–24
Steve (Kid) Sullivan		1924–25
Mike Ballerino		1925
Tod Morgan		1925–29
Benny Bass		1929–31
Kid Chocolate		1931–33
Frankie Klick		1933–34
Sandy Saddler (Claimant)		1949–50
Harold Gomes		1959–60
Gabriel (Flash) Elorde		1960–67
Yoshiaki Numata		1967
Hiroshi Kobayashi		1967–71
Rene Barrientos	(WBC)	1969–70
Yoshiaki Numata	(WBC)	1970–71
Alfredo Marcano		1971–72
Ricardo Arredondo	(WBC)	1971–74
Ben Villaflor		1972–73
Kuniaki Shibata		1973
Ben Villaflor		1973–76
Kuniaki Shibata	(WBC)	1974–75
Alfredo Escalera	(WBC)	1975–78
Samuel Serrano		1976–80
Alexis Arguello	(WBC)	1978–80
Yasutsune Uehara		1980–81
Rafael Limon	(WBC)	1980–81
Cornelius Boza-Edwards	(WBC)	1981
Samuel Serrano		1981–83
Rolando Navarrete	(WBC)	1981–82
Rafael Limon	(WBC)	1982
Bobby Chacon	(WBC)	1982–83

Champion	Organization	Year
Roger Mayweather		1983–84
Hector Camacho	(WBC)	1983–84
Rocky Lockridge		1984–85
Hwan-Kil Yuh	(IBF)	1984–85
Julio Cesar Chavez	(WBC)	1984–87
Lester Ellis	(IBF)	1985
Wilfredo Gomez		1985–86
Barry Michael	(IBF)	1985–87
Alfredo Layne		1986
Brian Mitchell		1986–91
Rocky Lockridge	(IBF)	1987–88
Azumah Nelson	(WBC)	1988–94
Tony Lopez	(IBF)	1988–89
Juan Molina	(IBF)	1989–90
Tony Lopez	(IBF)	1990–91
Joey Gamache	(WBA)	1991
Brian Mitchell	(IBF)	1991
Genaro Hernandez	(WBA)	1991–95
James Leija	(WBC)	1994
Juan Molina	(IBF)	1991–95
Gabriel Ruelas	(WBC)	1994–95
Eddie Hopson	(IBF)	1995
Tracy Patterson	(IBF)	1995
Azumah Nelson	(WBC)	1995–97
Choi Yong-Soo	(WBA)	1995–98
Arturo Gatti	(IBF)	1995–98
Genaro Hernandez	(WBC)	1997–98
Floyd Mayweather Jr.	(WBC)	1998–2002
Takanori Hatakeyama	(WBA)	1998–99
Roberto Garcia	(IBF)	1998–99
Lavka Sim	(WBA)	1999
Diego Corrales	(IBF)	1999–2001
Baek Jong-Kwon	(WBA)	1999–2000
Joel Casamayor	(WBA)	2000–02
Steve Forbes	(IBF)	2001–02
Acelino Freitas	(WBA)	2002–
Sirimongkol Singmanassak	(WBC)	2002–

Lightweight Champions (135 pounds)

Champion	Organization	Year
Jack McAuliffe		1886–94
George (Kid) Lavigne		1896–99
Frank Erne		1899–02
Joe Gans		1902–04
Jimmy Britt		1904–05
Battling Nelson		1905–06
Joe Gans		1906–08

Champion	Organization	Year	Champion	Organization	Year
Battling Nelson		1908–10	Esteban De Jesus	(WBC)	1976–78
Ad Wolgast		1910–12	Jim Watt	(WBC)	1979–81
Willie Ritchie		1912–14	Ernesto Espana	(WBA)	1979–80
Freddie Welsh		1915–17	Hilmer Kenty	(WBA)	1980–81
Benny Leonard		1917–25	Sean O'Grady	(WBA)	1981
Jimmy Goodrich		1925	Alexis Arguello	(WBC)	1981–82
Rocky Kansas		1925–26	Claude Noel	(WBA)	1981
Sammy Mandell		1926–30	Andrew Ganigan	(WBA)	1981–82
Al Singer		1930	Arturo Frias	(WBA)	1981–82
Tony Canzoneri		1930–33	Ray Mancini	(WBA)	1982–84
Barney Ross		1933–35	Alexis Arguello		1982–83
Tony Canzoneri		1935–36	Edwin Rosario	(WBC)	1983–84
Lou Ambers		1936–38	Choo Choo Brown	(IBF)	1984
Henry Armstrong		1938–39	Livingstone Bramble	(WBA)	1984–86
Lou Ambers		1939–40	Harry Arroyo	(IBF)	1984–85
Sammy Angott	(NBA)	1940–41	Jose Luis Ramirez	(WBC)	1984–85
Lew Jenkins		1940–41	Jimmy Paul	(IBF)	1985–86
Sammy Angott		1941–42	Hector Camacho	(WBC)	1985–86
Beau Jack		1942–43	Edwin Rosario	(WBA)	1986–87
Slugger White		1943	Greg Haugen	(IBF)	1986–87
Bob Montgomery		1943	Julio Cesar Chavez	(WBA)	1987–88
Sammy Angott	(NBA)	1943–44	Jose Luis Ramirez	(WBC)	1987–88
Beau Jack		1943–44	Julio Cesar Chavez	(WBC, WBA)	1988–89
Bob Montgomery		1944–47	Vinny Pazienza	(IBF)	1987–88
Juan Zurita	(NBA)	1944–45	Greg Haugen	(IBF)	1988–89
Ike Williams		1947–51	Pernell Whitaker	(IBF, WBC)	1989–90
James Carter		1951–52	Edwin Rosario	(WBA)	1989–90
Lauro Salas		1952	Juan Nazario	(WBA)	1990
James Carter		1952–54	Pernell Whitaker	(IBF, WBC, WBA)	1990–92
Paddy Demarco		1954	Joey Gamache	(WBA)	1992
James Carter		1954–55	Miguel A Gonzalez	(WBC)	1992–96
Wallace (Bud) Smith		1955–56	Tony Lopez	(WBA)	1992–93
Joe Brown		1956–62	Dingaan Thobela	(WBA)	1993
Carlos Ortiz		1962–65	Fred Pendleton	(IBF)	1993–94
Kenny Lane		1963–64	Orzubek Nazarov	(WBA)	1993–98
Ismael Laguna		1965	Rafael Ruelas	(IBF)	1994–95
Carlos Ortiz		1965–68	Oscar De La Hoya	(IBF)	1995
Carlos Teo Cruz		1968–69	Phillip Holiday	(IBF)	1995–97
Mando Ramos		1969–70	Jean-Baptiste Mendy	(WBC)	1996–97
Ismael Laguna		1970	Stevie Johnston	(WBC)	1997–98
Ken Buchanan		1970–72	Shane Mosley	(IBF)	1997–99
Pedro Carrasco	(WBC)	1971–72	Cesar Bazan	(WBC)	1998–99
Mando Ramos	(WBC)	1972	Jean-Baptiste Mendy	(WBA)	1998–99
Roberto Duran		1972–79	Julien Lorcy	(WBA)	1999
Chango Carmona	(WBC)	1972	Stevie Johnston	(WBC)	1999–2000
Rodolfo Gonzalez	(WBC)	1972–74	Stefano Zoff	(WBA)	1999
Ishimatsu Suzuki	(WBC)	1974–76	Israel Cardona	(IBF)	1999

Champion	Organization	Year
Paul Spadafora	(IBF)	1999–
Gilberto Serrano	(WBA)	1999–2000
Takanori Hatakeyama	(WBA)	2000–01
Jose Luis Castillo	(WBC)	2000–02
Julien Lorcy	(WBA)	2001
Raul Balbi	(WBA)	2001–02
Leonard Dorin	(WBA)	2002–
Floyd Mayweather	(WBC)	2002–

Junior Welterweight Champions (140 pounds)

Champion	Organization	Year
Pinkey Mitchell		1922–25
Red Herring		1925
Mushy Callahan		1926–30
Jack (Kid) Berg		1930–31
Tony Canzoneri		1931–32
Johnny Jadick		1932–33
Sammy Fuller		1932–33
Battling Shaw		1933
Tony Canzoneri		1933
Barney Ross		1933–35
Tippy Larkin		1946
Carlos Ortiz		1959–60
Duilio Loi		1960–62
Eddie Perkins		1962
Duilio Loi		1962–63
Roberto Cruz		1963
Eddie Perkins		1963–65
Carlos Hernandez		1965–66
Sandro Lopopolo		1966–67
Paul Fujii		1967–68
Nicolino Loche		1968–72
Pedro Adigue	(WBC)	1968–70
Bruno Arcari	(WBC)	1970–74
Alfonso Frazer		1972
Antonio Cervantes		1972–76
Perico Fernandez	(WBC)	1974–75
Saensak Muangsurin	(WBC)	1975–76
Wilfred Benitez		1976–79
Miguel Velasquez	(WBC)	1976
Saensak Muangsurin	(WBC)	1976–78
Antonio Cervantes	(WBA)	1977–80
Sang-Hyun Kim	(WBC)	1978–80
Saoul Mamby	(WBC)	1980–82

Champion	Organization	Year
Aaron Pryor	(WBA)	1980–83
Leroy Haley	(WBC)	1982–83
Aaron Pryor	(IBF)	1983–85
Bruce Curry	(WBC)	1983–84
Johnny Bumphus	(WBA)	1984
Bill Costello	(WBC)	1984–85
Gene Hatcher	(WBA)	1984–85
Ubaldo Sacco	(WBA)	1985–86
Lonnie Smith	(WBC)	1985–86
Patrizio Oliva	(WBA)	1986–87
Gary Hinton	(IBF)	1986
Rene Arredondo	(WBC)	1986
Tsuyoshi Hamada	(WBC)	1986–87
Joe Louis Manley	(IBF)	1986–87
Terry Marsh	(IBF)	1987
Juan Coggi	(WBA)	1987–90
Rene Arredondo	(WBC)	1987
Roger Mayweather	(WBC)	1987–89
James McGirt	(IBF)	1988
Meldrick Taylor	(IBF)	1988–90
Julio Cesar Chavez	(WBC)	1989–94
Julio Cesar Chavez	(IBF)	1990–91
Loreto Garza	(WBA)	1990–91
Juan Coggi	(WBA)	1991
Edwin Rosario	(WBA)	1991–92
Rafael Pineda	(IBF)	1991–92
Akinobu Hiranaka	(WBA)	1992
Pernell Whitaker	(IBF)	1992–93
Charles Murray	(IBF)	1993–94
Jake Rodriguez	(IBF)	1994–95
Juan Coggi	(WBA)	1993–94
Frankie Randall	(WBC)	1994
Frankie Randall	(WBA)	1994–96
Juan Coggi	(WBA)	1996
Julio Cesar Chavez	(WBC)	1994–96
Kostya Tszyu	(IBF)	1995–97
Frankie Randall	(WBA)	1996–97
Oscar De La Hoya	(WBC)	1996–97
Khalid Rahilou	(WBA)	1997–98
Vincent Phillips	(IBF)	1997–99
Sharmba Mitchell	(WBA)	1998–2001
Terronn Millet	(IBF)	1999–2000
Kostya Tszyu	(WBC)	1999–2000
Zab Judah	(IBF)	2000–01
Kostya Tszyu	(IBF, WBA, WBC)	2001–

Champion	Organization	Year	Champion	Organization	Year
Welterweight Champions (147 pounds)			Johnny Bratton		1951
			Kid Gavilan		1951–54
Paddy Duffy (Claimant)		1888–90	Johnny Saxton		1954–55
Mysterious Billy Smith		1892–94	Tony Demarco		1955
Tommy Ryan		1894–98	Carmen Basilio		1955–56
Mysterious Billy Smith		1898–1900	Johnny Saxton		1956
Matty Matthews		1900	Carmen Basilio		1956–57
Eddie Connolly		1900	Virgil Akins		1958
James (Rube) Ferns		1900	Don Jordan		1958–60
Matty Mathews		1900–01	Benny (Kid) Paret		1960–61
James (Rube) Ferns		1901	Emile Griffith		1961
Joe Walcott		1901–04	Benny (Kid) Paret		1961–62
The Dixie Kid		1904–05	Emile Griffith		1962–63
Honey Mellody		1906–07	Luis Rodriguez		1963
Mike (Twin) Sullivan		1907–08	Emile Griffith		1963–66
Harry Lewis		1908–11	Charlie Shipes		1966–67
Jimmy Gardner		1908	Curtis Cokes		1966–69
Jimmy Clabby		1910–11	Jose Napoles		1969–70
Waldemar Holberg		1914	Billy Backus		1970–71
Tom McCormick		1914	Jose Napoles		1971–75
Matt Wells		1914–15	Hedgemon Lewis		1972–73
Mike Glover		1915	Angel Espada	(WBA)	1975–76
Jack Britton		1915	John H. Stracey		1975–76
Ted (Kid) Lewis		1915–16	Carlos Palomino		1976–79
Jack Britton		1916–17	Pipino Cuevas	(WBA)	1976–80
Ted (Kid) Lewis		1917–19	Wilfredo Benitez		1979
Jack Britton		1919–22	Sugar Ray Leonard		1979–80
Mickey Walker		1922–26	Roberto Duran		1980
Pete Latzo		1926–27	Thomas Hearns	(WBA)	1980–81
Joe Dundee		1927–29	Sugar Ray Leonard		1980–82
Jackie Fields		1929–30	Donald Curry	(WBA)	1983–85
Young Jack Thompson		1930	Milton McCrory	(WBC)	1983–85
Tommy Freeman		1930–31	Donald Curry		1985–86
Young Jack Thompson		1931	Lloyd Honeyghan		1986–87
Lou Brouillard		1931–32	Jorge Vaca	(WBC)	1987–88
Jackie Fields		1932–33	Lloyd Honeyghan	(WBC)	1988–89
Young Corbett II		1933	Mark Breland	(WBA)	1987
Jimmy McLarnin		1933–34	Marlon Starling	(WBA)	1987–88
Barney Ross		1934	Tomas Molinares	(WBA)	1988–89
Jimmy McLarnin		1934–35	Simon Brown	(IBF)	1988–91
Barney Ross		1935–38	Mark Breland	(WBA)	1989–90
Henry Armstrong		1938–40	Marlon Starling	(WBC)	1989–90
Fritzie Zivic		1940–41	Aaron Davis	(WBA)	1990–91
Izzy Jannazzo	(Md.)	1940–41	Maurice Blocker	(WBC)	1990–91
Freddie (Red) Cochrane		1941–46	Meldrick Taylor	(WBA)	1991–92
Marty Servo		1946	Simon Brown	(WBC)	1991
Sugar Ray Robinson		1946–51	Maurice Blocker	(IBF)	1991–93

Champion	Organization	Year	Champion	Organization	Year
Buddy McGirt	(WBC)	1991–93	Mark Medal	(IBF)	1984
Crisanto Espana	(WBA)	1992–94	Thomas Hearns		1984–86
Pernell Whitaker	(WBC)	1993–97	Mike McCallum	(WBA)	1984–87
Felix Trinidad	(IBF)	1993–99	Carlos Santos	(IBF)	1984–86
Ike Quartey	(WBA)	1994–98	Buster Drayton	(IBF)	1986–87
James Page	(WBA)	1998–2000	Duane Thomas	(WBC)	1986–87
Oscar De La Hoya	(WBC)	1997–99	Matthew Hilton	(IBF)	1987–88
Felix Trinidad	(WBC, IBF)	1999–2000	Lupe Aquino	(WBC)	1987
Oscar De La Hoya	(WBC)	2000	Gianfranco Rosi	(WBC)	1987–88
Shane Mosley	(WBC)	2000–02	Julian Jackson	(WBA)	1987–90
Andrew Lewis	(WBA)	2001–02	Donald Curry	(WBC)	1988–89
Vernon Forrest		2001–02	Robert Hines	(IBF)	1988–89
Vernon Forrest	(WBC)	2002–	Darrin Van Horn	(IBF)	1989
			Rene Jacquote	(WBC)	1989

Junior Middleweight Champions (154 pounds)

Champion	Organization	Year	Champion	Organization	Year
			John Mugabi	(WBC)	1989–90
			Gianfranco Rosi	(IBF)	1989–94
Emile Griffith		1962–63	Terry Norris	(WBC)	1990–94
Dennis Moyer		1962–63	Gilbert Dele	(WBA)	1991
Ralph Dupas		1963	Vinny Pazienza	(WBA)	1991–92
Sandro Mazzinghi		1963–65	Julio Cesar Vasquez	(WBA)	1992–95
Nino Benvenuti		1965–66	Simon Brown	(WBC)	1994
Ki-Soo Kim		1966–68	Terry Norris	(WBC)	1994–
Sandro Mazzinghi		1968	Vincent Pettway	(IBF)	1994–95
Freddie Little		1969–70	Paul Vaden	(IBF)	1995
Carmelo Bossi		1970–71	Carl Daniels	(WBA)	1995
Koichi Wajima		1971–74	Terry Norris	(WBC)	1995–97
Oscar Albarado		1974–75	Terry Norris	(IBF)	1995–96
Koichi Wajima		1975	Laurent Boudouani	(WBA)	1996–99
Miguel De Oliveira	(WBC)	1975–76	Raul Marquez	(IBF)	1997
Jae-Do Yuh		1975–76	Keith Mullings	(WBC)	1997–99
Elisha Obed	(WBC)	1975–76	Yori Boy Campas	(IBF)	1997–98
Koichi Wajima		1976	Fernando Vargas	(IBF)	1998–2000
Jose Duran		1976	Javier Castillejo	(WBC)	1999–2001
Eckhard Dagge	(WBC)	1976–77	David Reid	(WBA)	1999–2000
Miguel Angel Castellini		1976–77	Felix Trinidad	(WBA, IBF)	2000–01
Eddie Gazo		1977–78	Oscar De La Hoya	(WBC)	2001–
Rocky Mattioli	(WBC)	1977–79	Fernando Vargas	(WBA)	2001–02
Masashi Kudo		1978–79	Ronald Wright	(IBF)	2001–
Maurice Hope	(WBC)	1979–81	Oscar De La Hoya	(WBA, WBC)	2002–
Ayub Kalule		1979–81			

Middleweight Champions (160 pounds)

Champion	Organization	Year	Champion	Year
Wilfred Benitez	(WBC)	1981–82	Jack (Nonpareil) Dempsey	1884–91
Sugar Ray Leonard		1981–82	Bob Fitzsimmons	1891–97
Tadashi Mihara	(WBA)	1981–82	Charles (Kid) McCoy	1897–98
Davey Moore	(WBA)	1982–83	Tommy Ryan	1898–1907
Thomas Hearns	(WBC)	1982–84	Stanley Ketchel	1908
Roberto Duran	(WBA)	1983–84		

Champion	Organization	Year	Champion	Organization	Year
Billy Papke		1908	Carmen Basilio		1957–58
Stanley Ketchel		1908–10	Sugar Ray Robinson		1958–60
Frank Klaus		1913	Gene Fullmer	(NBA)	1959–62
George Chip		1913–14	Paul Pender		1960–61
Al McCoy		1914–17	Terry Downes		1961–62
Jeff Smith		1914	Paul Pender		1962–63
Mick King		1914	Dick Tiger	(WBA)	1962–63
Jeff Smith		1914–15	Dick Tiger		1963
Lee Darcy		1915–17	Joey Giardello		1963–65
Mike O'Dowd		1917–20	Dick Tiger		1965–66
Johnny Wilson		1920–23	Emile Griffith		1966–67
Wm. Bryan Downey		1921–22	Nino Benvenuti		1967
Dave Rosenberg		1922	Emile Griffith		1967–68
Jock Malone		1922–23	Nino Benvenuti		1968–70
Mike O'Dowd		1922	Carlos Monzon		1970–77
Lou Bogash		1923	Rodrigo Valdez	(WBC)	1974–76
Harry Greb		1923–26	Rodrigo Valdez		1977–78
Tiger Flowers		1926	Hugo Corro		1978–79
Mickey Walker		1926–31	Vito Antuofermo		1979–80
Gorilla Jones		1931–32	Alan Minter		1980
Marcel Thil		1932–37	Marvelous Marvin Hagler		1980–87
Ben Jeby		1932–33	Sugar Ray Leonard		1987
Lou Brouillard	(NBA)	1933	Frank Tate	(IBF)	1987–88
Vince Dundee	(NBA)	1933–34	Sumbu Kalambay	(WBA)	1987–89
Teddy Yarosz	(NBA)	1934–35	Thomas Hearns	(WBC)	1987–88
Babe Risko	(NBA)	1935–36	Iran Barkley	(WBC)	1988–89
Freddie Steele	(NBA)	1936–38	Michael Nunn	(IBF)	1988–91
Fred Apostoli		1937–39	Roberto Duran	(WBC)	1989–90
Al Hostak	(NBA)	1938	Mike McCallum	(WBA)	1989–91
Solly Krieger	(NBA)	1938–39	Julian Jackson	(WBC)	1990–93
Al Hostak	(NBA)	1939–40	James Toney	(IBF)	1991–93
Ceferino Garcia		1939–40	Reggie Johnson	(WBA)	1992–93
Ken Overlin		1940–41	Roy Jones Jr.	(IBF)	1993–94
Tony Zale	(NBA)	1940–41	Gerald McClellan	(WBC)	1993–95
Billy Soose		1941	John David Jackson	(WBA)	1993–94
Tony Zale		1941–47	Jorge Castro	(WBA)	1994–97
Rocky Graziano		1947–48	Julian Jackson	(WBC)	1995
Tony Zale		1948	Bernard Hopkins	(IBF)	1995–00
Marcel Cerdan		1948–49	Quincy Taylor	(WBC)	1995–96
Jake La Motta		1949–51	Shinji Takehara	(WBA)	1995–96
Sugar Ray Robinson		1951	William Joppy	(WBA)	1996–97
Randy Turpin		1951	Keith Holmes	(WBC)	1996–98
Sugar Ray Robinson		1951–52	Julio Cesar Green	(WBA)	1997–98
Carl (Bobo) Olson		1953–55	William Joppy	(WBA)	1998–2001
Sugar Ray Robinson		1955–57	Hassine Cherifi	(WBC)	1998–99
Gene Fullmer		1957	Keith Holmes	(WBC)	1999–2001
Sugar Ray Robinson		1957	Bernard Hopkins	(IBF, WBC)	2001–

Champion	Organization	Year
Felix Trinidad	(WBA)	2001
Bernard Hopkins	(IBF, WBA, WBC)	2001–

Super Middleweight Champions (167 pounds)

Champion	Organization	Year
Murray Sutherland	(IBF)	1984
Chong-Pal Park	(IBF)	1984–87
Chong-Pal Park	(WBA)	1987–88
Graziano Rocchigiani	(IBF)	1988–89
Fugencio Obelmejias	(WBA)	1988–89
Ray Leonard	(WBC)	1988–90
In-Chut Baek	(WBA)	1989–90
Lindell Holmes	(IBF)	1990–91
Christophe Tiozzo	(WBA)	1990–91
Mauro Galvano	(WBC)	1990–92
Victor Cordova	(WBA)	1991
Darrin Van Horn	(IBF)	1991–92
Iran Barkley	(WBA)	1992
Nigel Benn	(WBC)	1992–96
James Toney	(IBF)	1992–94
Michael Nunn	(WBA)	1992–94
Steve Little	(WBA)	1994
Frank Liles	(WBA)	1994–99
Roy Jones	(IBF)	1994–96
Thulane Malinga	(WBC)	1996
Vincenzo Nardiello	(WBC)	1996
Robin Reid	(WBC)	1996–97
Charles Brewer	(IBF)	1997–98
Sven Ottke	(IBF)	1998–
Thulane Malinga	(WBC)	1997–98
Richie Woodhall	(WBC)	1998–99
Byron Mitchell	(WBA)	1999–2000
Markus Beyer	(WBC)	1999–2000
Glenn Gatley	(WBC)	2000
Dingaan Thobela	(WBC)	2000
Bruno Girard	(WBA)	2000–01
Dave Hilton	(WBC)	2000
Byron Mitchell	(WBA)	2001–
Eric Lucas	(WBC)	2001–

Light Heavyweight Champions (118 pounds)

Champion	Organization	Year
Jack Root		1903
George Gardner		1903
Bob Fitzsimmons		1903–05

Champion	Organization	Year
Philadelphia Jack O'Brien		1905–12
Jack Dillon		1914–16
Battling Levinsky		1916–20
Georges Carpentier		1920–22
Battling Siki		1922–23
Mike McTigue		1923–25
Paul Berlenbach		1925–26
Jack Delaney		1926–27
Jimmy Slattery	(NBA)	1927
Tommy Loughran		1927–29
Jimmy Slattery		1930
Maxie Rosenbloom		1930–34
George Nichols	(NBA)	1932
Bob Godwin	(NBA)	1933
Bob Olin		1934–35
John Henry Lewis		1935–38
Melio Bettina		1939
Len Harvey		1939–42
Billy Conn		1939–40
Anton Christoforidis	(NBA)	1941
Gus Lesnevich		1941–48
Freddie Mills		1942–46
Freddie Mills		1948–50
Joey Maxim		1950–52
Archie Moore		1952–62
Harold Johnson	(NBA)	1961
Harold Johnson		1962–63
Willie Pastrano		1963–65
Eddie Cotton		1963–64
Jose Torres		1965–66
Dick Tiger		1966–68
Bob Foster		1968–74
Vicente Rondon	(WBA)	1971–72
John Conteh	(WBC)	1974–77
Victor Galindez	(WBA)	1974–78
Miguel A. Cuello	(WBC)	1977–78
Mate Parlov	(WBC)	1978
Mike Rossman	(WBA)	1978–79
Marvin Johnson	(WBC)	1978–79
Matthew (Franklin) Saad Muhammad	(WBC)	1979–81
Marvin Johnson	(WBA)	1979–80
Eddie (Gregory) Mustapha Muhammad	(WBA)	1980–81
Michael Spinks	(WBA)	1981–83
Dwight (Braxton) Muhammad Qawi	(WBC)	1981–83

Champion	Organization	Year	Champion	Organization	Year
Michael Spinks		1983–85	Evander Holyfield	(WBA)	1986–88
J.B.Williamson	(WBC)	1985–86	Ricky Parkey	(IBF)	1986–87
Slobodan Kacar	(IBF)	1985–86	Evander Holyfield	(WBA, IBF)	1987–88
Marvin Johnson	(WBA)	1986–87	Evander Holyfield		1988
Dennis Andries	(WBC)	1986–87	Toufik Belbouli	(WBA)	1989
Bobby Czyz	(IBF)	1986–87	Robert Daniels	(WBA)	1989–91
Leslie Stewart	(WBA)	1987	Carlos De Leon	(WBC)	1989–90
Virgil Hill	(WBA)	1987–91	Glenn McCrory	(IBF)	1989–90
Prince Charles Williams	(IBF)	1987–93	Jeff Lampkin	(IBF)	1990
Thomas Hearns	(WBC)	1987	Massimiliano Duran	(WBC)	1990–91
Donny Lalonde	(WBC)	1987–88	Bobby Czyz	(WBA)	1991–92
Sugar Ray Leonard	(WBC)	1988	Anaclet Wamba	(WBC)	1991–95
Dennis Andries	(WBC)	1989	James Pritchard	(IBF)	1991
Jeff Harding	(WBC)	1989–90	James Warring	(IBF)	1991–92
Dennis Andries	(WBC)	1990–91	Alfred Cole	(IBF)	1992–96
Jeff Harding	(WBC)	1991–94	Orlin Norris	(WBA)	1993–95
Thomas Hearns	(WBA)	1991–92	Nate Miller	(WBA)	1995–97
Iran Barkley	(WBA)	1992	Marcelo Dominguez	(WBC)	1996–98
Virgil Hill	(WBA)	1992–97	Adolpho Washington	(IBF)	1996–97
Henry Maske	(IBF)	1993–96	Uriah Grant	(IBF)	1997
Virgil Hill	(WBA, IBF)	1996–97	Imamu Mayfield	(IBF)	1997–98
Mike McCallum	(WBC)	1994–95	Arthur Williams	(IBF)	1998–99
Fabrice Tiozzo	(WBC)	1995–96	Fabrice Tiozzo	(WBA)	1997–2000
Roy Jones Jr.	(WBC)	1996	Juan Carlos Gomez	(WBC)	1998–2002
Montell Griffin	(WBC)	1996	Vassiliy Jirov	(IBF)	1999–2000
D. Michaelczewski	(WBA, IBF)	1997	Virgil Hill	(WBA)	2000–02
William Guthrie	(IBF)	1997–98	Jean-Marc Mormeck	(WBA)	2002–
Lou Del Valle	(WBA)	1997–98	Wayne Braithwaite	(WBC)	2002–
Roy Jones Jr.	(WBA, WBC)	1997–2000			
Reggie Johnson	(IBF)	1998–99			
Roy Jones Jr.	(WBA, WBC, IBF)	1999–2000			

Cruiserweight Champions (195 pounds)

Marvin Camel	(WBC)	1980
Carlos De Leon	(WBC)	1980–82
Ossie Ocasio	(WBA)	1982–84
S.T. Gordon	(WBC)	1982–83
Carlos De Leon	(WBC)	1983–85
Marvin Camel	(IBF)	1983–84
Lee Roy Murphy	(IBF)	1984–86
Piet Crous	(WBA)	1984–85
Alfonso Ratliff	(WBC)	1985
Dwight Braxton	(WBA)	1985–86
Bernard Benton	(WBC)	1985–86
Carlos De Leon	(WBC)	1986–88

Heavyweight Champions (over 190 pounds)

John L. Sullivan	1885–92
James J. Corbett	1892–97
Bob Fitzsimmons	1897–99
James J. Jeffries	1899–1905
Marvin Hart	1905–06
Tommy Burns	1906–08
Jack Johnson	1908–15
Jess Willard	1915–19
Jack Dempsey	1919–26
Gene Tunney	1926–28
Max Schmeling	1930–32
Jack Sharkey	1932–33
Primo Carnera	1933–34
Max Baer	1934–35
James J. Braddock	1935–37

Champion	Organization	Year	Champion	Organization	Year
Joe Louis		1937–49	Tim Witherspoon	(WBA)	1986
Ezzard Charles		1949–51	Trevor Berbick	(WBC)	1986
Jersey Joe Walcott		1951–52	Mike Tyson	(WBC)	1986–87
Rocky Marciano		1952–56	James (Bonecrusher) Smith	(WBA)	1986–87
Floyd Patterson		1956–59	Tony Tucker	(IBF)	1987
Ingemar Johansson		1959–60	Mike Tyson	(WBC, WBA, IBF)	1987–90
Floyd Patterson		1960–62	Buster Douglas	(WBC, WBA, IBF)	1990
Sonny Liston		1962–64	Evander Holyfield	(WBC, WBA, IBF)	1990–92
Cassius Clay (Muhammad Ali)		1964–67	Riddick Bowe	(WBA, IBF)	1992–93
Ernie Terrell	(WBA)	1965–67	Lennox Lewis	(WBC)	1992–94
Joe Frazier		1968–70	Evander Holyfield	(WBA, IBF)	1993–94
Jimmy Ellis	(WBA)	1968–70	Michael Moorer	(WBA, IBF)	1994
Joe Frazier		1970–73	Oliver McCall	(WBC)	1994–95
George Foreman		1973–74	George Foreman	(WBA, IBF)	1994–95
Muhammad Ali		1974–78	Bruce Seldon	(WBA)	1995–96
Leon Spinks		1978	George Foreman		1995–96
Ken Norton	(WBC)	1978	Frank Bruno	(WBC)	1995–96
Larry Holmes	(WBC)	1978–80	Mike Tyson	(WBC)	1996
Muhammad Ali		1978–79	Mike Tyson	(WBA)	1996
John Tate	(WBA)	1979–80	Michael Moorer	(IBF)	1996–1997
Mike Weaver	(WBA)	1980–82	Evander Holyfield	(WBA, IBF)	1996–2000
Larry Holmes		1980–85	Lennox Lewis	(WBC)	1997–2000
Michael Dokes	(WBA)	1982–83	Lennox Lewis	(WBA, WBC, IBF)	2000
Gerrie Coetzee	(WBA)	1983–84	Evander Holyfield	(WBA)	2000–01
Tim Witherspoon	(WBC)	1984	Lennox Lewis	(WBC, IBF)	2000–01
Pinklon Thomas	(WBC)	1984–86	John Ruiz	(WBA)	2001–
Greg Page	(WBA)	1984–85	Hasim Rahman	(WBC, IBF)	2001
Michael Spinks		1985–87	Lennox Lewis	(WBC, IBF)	2001–

Notes

Introduction: The Sweet Science

1. Quoted in Gregory Crosby, "Tales of Vegas Past: The Sweet (and Sour) Science," *Las Vegas Mercury*, September 19, 2002.
2. Quoted in Crosby, "Tales of Vegas Past."
3. Quoted in Monte Cox, "Boxing: The Theater of the Unexpected!" Cox's Corner. http://coxscorner.tripod.com.

Chapter 1: Warriors All

4. Quoted in Harry Carpenter, *Boxing: An Illustrated History.* New York: Crescent, 1982, p. 8.
5. Quoted in Peter Arnold, *History of Boxing.* Secaucus, NJ: Chartwell, 1985, p. 9.
6. Quoted in The International Boxing Hall of Fame website. www.ibhof.com.
7. Arnold, *History of Boxing*, p. 12.
8. Quoted in Carpenter, *Boxing*, p. 13.
9. Quoted in Arnold, *History of Boxing*, p. 13.
10. Quoted in Arnold, *History of Boxing*, p. 17.

11. Quoted in The International Boxing Hall of Fame website.

Chapter 2: The Queensberry Rules

12. Quoted in Arnold, *History of Boxing*, pp. 34–35.
13. Quoted in Carpenter, *Boxing*, p. 27.
14. Quoted in Arnold, *History of Boxing*, p. 44.
15. Quoted in Carpenter, *Boxing*, p. 64.
16. Quoted in *San Francisco Examiner*, "Sharkey, Heavyweight Champ of Old," August 19, 1994, p. A-21.

Chapter 3: Into the Modern Era

17. James P. Dawson, "Marciano Annexes Title in 13th by KO over Joe Walcott," *New York Times*, September 24, 1952.
18. Quoted in Steve Farhood, "20th Century Boxing Myths," *Boxing Monthly*, December 1999. www.boxing.monthly.co.uk.
19. Quoted in *New York Times*, "LaMotta

Confesses He Threw '47 Garden Bout with Billy Fox," June 15, 1960.

20. Quoted in *New York Times*, "Carbo, 4 Others Are Found Guilty," May 31, 1961.

21. Quoted in Joyce Carol Oates, *On Boxing*. Garden City, NY: Dolphin/ Doubleday, 1987, p. 25.

22. Quoted in Anthony York, "'I Want to Eat Your Children. Praise Be to Allah,'" *Salon*, June 28, 2000. http://dir.salon.com.

Chapter 4: The Gladiators

23. Oates, *On Boxing*, p. 6.

24. Quoted in Carpenter, *Boxing*, p. 45.

25. Quoted in Larry Schwartz, "Defeats Didn't Dampen Dempsey," ESPN. espn.go.com.

26. Quoted in Mark G. Butcher, "Henry Armstrong—Former World Featherweight, Lightweight, and Welterweight Champion," Seconds Out. www.secondsout.com.

27. Quoted in B.R. Bearden, "Archie Moore's Remarkable Run at the Heavyweight Championship," East Side Boxing. www.eastsideboxing.com.

28. Quoted in Nicholas J. Cotsonika, "When Joe Louis Fought, the Country Came to a Halt," *Detroit Free Press*. www.freep.com.

29. Quoted in Ron Flatter, "The Sugar in the Sweet Science," ESPN.

http://espn.go.com.

30. Quoted in Flatter, "The Sugar in the Sweet Science."

31. Quoted in Larry Schwartz, "He Is Simply...The Greatest," ESPN. http://espn. go.com.

Chapter 5: The Spectacles

32. Oates, *On Boxing*, p. 8.

33. Quoted in Nat Fleischer and Sam Andre, *An Illustrated History of Boxing*. New York: Citadel, 2001, p. 46.

34. Quoted in CBS SportsLine, "Corbett vs. Sullivan." cbs.sportsline.com.

35. Quoted in Seconds Out, "Dempsey-Firpo: A Slugfest for the Ages." www.secondsout.com.

36. B.R. Bearden, "The Time Tunnel: 75th Anniversary of 'The Long Count,'" East Side Boxing. www. eastsideboxing.com.

37. Quoted in Bearden, "The Time Tunnel."

38. Quoted in CBS SportsLine, "Louis vs. Schmeling II." cbs.sportsline.com

39. Quoted in Carpenter, *Boxing*, p. 90.

40. Quoted in Monte Cox, "Fight of the Decade: 1940–1949," Cox's Corner. http://members.tripod.com.

41. Quoted in Mark Kram, "'Lawdy, Lawdy, He's Great,'" CNN/Sports Illustrated. http://sportsillustrated. cnn.com.

42. Quoted in Larry Schwartz, "'Thrilla in Manila' Was Epic Bout," ESPN. http://espn.go.com.

Chapter 6: Down for the Count?

43. Richard Hoffer, "Fight-Game Inferno," *Sports Illustrated*, March 10, 2003, p. 38.
44. Quoted in Allen Barra, "The Sweet Science," *Inside Sports*, February 1987, p. 73.
45. Quoted in Jack Newfield, "The Shame of Boxing," *Nation*, October 25, 2001.
46. Quoted in John Rawling, "Boxing Braced for Renewed Attack," *Guardian Unlimited*, December 18, 2000. www.guardian.co.uk
47. Patrick B. Fife, "The National Boxing Commission Act of 2001: It's Time for Congress to Step into the Ring and Save the Sport of Boxing," *Hofstra Law Review*, vol. 30, no. 4, Summer 2002, p. 1,305.
48. Newfield, "The Shame of Boxing."
49. Quoted in Tim Graham, "New WBO Division: Dead Weight," ESPN, February 20, 2001. http://espn.go.com.
50. Quoted in Hoffer, "Fight-Game Inferno," p. 42.
51. Newfield, "The Shame of Boxing."
52. Quoted in Newfield, "The Shame of Boxing."
53. Quoted in Richard Hoffer, "Up from the Canvas," *Sports Illustrated*, March 27, 1995, p. 54.
54. Quoted in Jeff Ryan, "Down for the Count," *Inside Sports*, December 1996, p. 80.
55. Quoted in Hoffer, "Fight-Game Inferno," p. 42.
56. Quoted in Ryan, "Down for the Count," p. 78.

For Further Reading

Books

Richard Bak, *Joe Louis: The Great Black Hope.* Dallas: Taylor, 1996. The biography of one of boxing's all-time great champions.

Michael T. Isenberg, *John L. Sullivan and His America.* Champaign: University of Illinois Press, 1994. A biography of the nation's first great boxing hero and the times in which he lived.

Bob Mee, *Bare Fists: The History of Bare-Knuckle Prize-Fighting.* New York: Overlook, 2001. A history of bare-knuckle boxing from the past up through the present day.

James P. Roberts and Alexander G. Skutt, *The Boxing Register.* 3rd ed. Ithaca, NY: McBooks, 2002. A carefully researched guide to boxing that includes biographical information on more than one hundred boxing figures.

Jeff Silverman, ed., *The Greatest Boxing Stories Ever Told.* New York: Lyons, 2002. A collection of some of the most memorable writings on the sweet science.

Russell Sullivan, *Rocky Marciano: The Rock of the Times.* Champaign: University of Illinois Press, 2002. The biography of history's only undefeated heavyweight boxing champion.

Websites

International Boxing Federation (www.ibf-usba-boxing.com). The official website of the IBF.

USA Boxing (www.usaboxing.org). The official website of the national governing body of amateur boxing in the United States.

World Boxing Association (www.wbaonline.com). The official website of the WBA.

World Boxing Organization (www.wbo-int.com). The official website of the WBO.

Works Consulted

Books

Peter Arnold, *History of Boxing.* Secaucus, NJ: Chartwell, 1985. Arnold's history includes a chapter on great boxers and great ring battles.

Gene Brown, ed., *The New York Times Encyclopedia of Sports: Boxing.* New York: Arno, 1979. The evolution of boxing is traced through newspaper articles dealing with significant events in the sport's history.

Harry Carpenter, *Boxing: An Illustrated History.* New York: Crescent, 1982. In addition to many full-color photos, this history also includes a listing of professional and Olympic champions through 1982.

Nat Fleischer and Sam Andre, *An Illustrated History of Boxing.* New York: Citadel, 2001. A lavishly illustrated history of the sport from the time of James Figg.

Ford Hovis, ed., *The Sports Encyclopedia.* New York: Rutledge, 1976. This comprehensive volume describes the history, rules, equipment, and game techniques and strategy involved in fifty-six sports.

Joyce Carol Oates, *On Boxing.* Garden City, NY: Dolphin/Doubleday, 1987. A look at boxing from the point of view of one of the most popular and respected novelists of the modern day.

Periodicals

Bob Barnett, "Coming to Scratch," *Sports Heritage,* July/August 1987.

Allen Barra, "The Sweet Science," *Inside Sports,* February 1987.

Gregory Crosby, "Tales of Vegas Past: The Sweet (and Sour) Science," *Las Vegas Mercury,* September 19, 2002.

James P. Dawson, "Marciano Annexes Title in 13th by KO over Joe Walcott," *New York Times,* September 24, 1952.

Patrick B. Fife, "The National Boxing Commission Act of 2001: It's Time for Congress to Step into the Ring and Save the Sport of Boxing," *Hofstra Law Review,* vol. 30, no. 4, Summer 2002.

Stedman Graham, "Boxing Can't Heal

Itself," *Inside Sports*, November 1997.

———, "The Brutal Truth of Boxing," *Inside Sports*, November 1995.

Richard Hoffer, "Fight-Game Inferno," *Sports Illustrated*, March 10, 2003.

———, "Up from the Canvas," *Sports Illustrated*, March 27, 1995.

Robert Horn, "Belting the Champions," *Sports Illustrated*, April 4, 1994.

Jack Newfield, "The Shame of Boxing," *Nation*, October 25, 2001.

New York Times, "Carbo, 4 Others Are Found Guilty," May 31, 1961.

———, "LaMotta Confesses He Threw '47 Garden Bout with Billy Fox," June 15, 1960.

Jeff Ryan, "Down for the Count," *Inside Sports*, December 1996.

San Francisco Examiner, "Sharkey, Heavyweight Champ of Old," August 19, 1994.

Internet Sources

B.R. Bearden, "Archie Moore's Remarkable Run at the Heavyweight Championship," East Side Boxing. www.eastsideboxing.com.

———, "The Time Tunnel: 75th Anniversary of 'The Long Count,'" East Side Boxing. www.eastsideboxing.com.

Angelo Bruscas, "Rademacher, 72, Still in There Swinging for Olympic Ideal," *Seattle Post-Intelligence*, August 25, 2000. www.seattlepi.nwsource.com.

Mark G. Butcher, "Henry Armstrong—

Former World Featherweight, Lightweight, and Welterweight Champion," Seconds Out. www.secondsout.com.

CBS SportsLine, "Corbett vs. Sullivan." www.cbs.sportsline.com.

———, "Louis vs. Schmeling II," http://cbs.sportsline.com.

Nicholas J. Cotsonika, "When Joe Louis Fought, the Country Came to a Halt," *Detroit Free Press*. www.freep.com.

Monte Cox, "Boxing: The Theater of the Unexpected!" Cox's Corner. http://coxscorner.tripod.com.

———, "Fight of the Decade: 1940–1949," Cox's Corner. http://members.tripod.com.

Steve Farhood, "20th Century Boxing Myths," *Boxing Monthly*, December 1999. www.boxing.monthly.co.uk.

Ron Flatter, "The Sugar in the Sweet Science," ESPN. http://espn.go.com.

Tim Graham, "New WBO Division: Dead Weight," ESPN, February 20, 2001. http://espn.go.com.

Mark Kram, "'Lawdy, Lawdy, He's Great,'" CNN/Sports Illustrated. http://sportsillustrated.cnn.com.

Eugene Robinson, "The Cuban Ali," *Observer*, February 3, 2002. www.guardian.co.uk.

John Rawling, "Boxing Braced for Renewed Attack," *Guardian Unlimited*, December 18, 2000. www.guardian.co.uk.

Larry Schwartz, "Defeats Didn't Dampen Dempsey," ESPN. espn.go.com.

———, "He Is Simply . . . The Greatest,"

ESPN. http:// espn.go.com.

———, "'Thrilla in Manila' Was Epic Bout," ESPN. http://espn.go.com.

Seconds Out. "Dempsey-Firpo: A Slugfest for the Ages," www.secondsout.com.

Anthony York, "'I Want to Eat Your Children. Praise Be to Allah,'" *Salon*, June 28, 2000. http://dir.salon.com.

Websites

The International Boxing Hall of Fame (www.ibhof.com). The official website of the International Boxing Hall of Fame in Canastota, New York.

Index

Picture Credits

Cover: Sports Imagery/Landov
American Pastime Sports, 60
AP/Wide World Photo, 77
© AFP/CORBIS, 44
© Bettmann/CORBIS , 9, 15, 29, 31, 33, 41, 45, 51, 63, 64,67,71
© Michael Brennan/CORBIS, 42
Brown Brothers, 20, 26, 36, 39, 48, 55, 56, 73
Hulton Archive by Getty Images, 16, 19, 23, 52, 79
© Scala/Art Resource, NY,11

About the Author

John F. Grabowski is a native of Brooklyn, New York. He holds a bachelor's degree in psychology from City College of New York and a master's degree in educational psychology from Teacher's College, Columbia University. He has been a teacher for thirty-three years, as well as a freelance writer, specializing in the fields of sports, education, and comedy. His body of published work includes forty-five books; a nationally syndicated sports column; consultation on several math textbooks; articles for newspapers, magazines, and the programs of professional sports teams; and comedy material sold to Jay Leno, Joan Rivers, Yakov Smirnoff, and numerous other comics. He and his wife, Patricia, live in Staten Island with their daughter, Elizabeth.